"This book will inspire and empower women—and their allies—at all levels of leadership to think bigger and intentionally about their professional impact and possibilities."

> **—DORIE CLARK,** *Wall Street Journal* bestselling author of *The Long Game* and executive education faculty at the Duke University Fuqua School of Business

"This book captures insightful and practical lessons that all aspiring leaders can learn from."

> **—JOHN DONAHOE,** CEO of Nike

"There are so many reasons to read this book: It is practical, poignant, personal, powerful, and pointed toward doing. The lessons learned from experience and research are provided in accessible ways. The authors are generous in sharing their favorite tools and best advice in the journey of moving beyond arriving to thriving. A must-read leadership resource."

> **—BARRY Z. POSNER, PhD,** Michael J. Accolti, S.J. Chair and Professor of Leadership, Chair of the Department of Management and Entrepreneurship at the Leavey School of Business, Santa Clara University

"If you are contemplating stepping up and stepping in, *even more*, the seven impactful practices in this book—and the wisdom of the three authors and the experts they highlight—will show you how."

> **—MOLLY FLETCHER,** speaker, author, former sports agent

"*Arrive and Thrive* is rooted in real world experience and incredible life lessons. The seven impactful practices have proven true throughout my leadership journey and reflect lessons that I learned both on the court and in the boardroom. In an era where so many of us think we are just surviving in this complex business world, this book will inspire you to move from survive to thrive."

—**CATHY ENGELBERT,** WNBA Commissioner

"Timely and pragmatic . . . this progress in gender equity and leadership will alter the trajectory of our society."

—**MICHAEL CROW,** president,
Arizona State University

"Bravo to this trio of authors who, leveraging their powerful and distinct leadership experiences, perspectives, and network bring us closer to understanding the essence of authentic leadership. This book is chock full of inspiration and tangible lessons for being our best and truest self."

—**ERIKA H. JAMES,** Dean of Wharton School
of the University of Pennsylvania

"Women fighting for gender equality have to upend so many barriers; a world of work built for men and outdated stereotypes. It can be exhausting but there is energy to be found in learning from the insights of *Arrive and Thrive*."

—**JULIA GILLARD,** 27th prime minister of Australia;
Chair of the Global Institute for Women's
Leadership, King's College London and the
Australian National University

# ARRIVE *and* THRIVE

# ARRIVE *and* THRIVE

## 7 Impactful Practices for Women Navigating Leadership

**Susan MacKenty Brady**
**Janet Foutty**
**Lynn Perry Wooten**

Mc
Graw
Hill

New York   Chicago   San Francisco   Athens   London   Madrid
Mexico City   Milan   New Delhi   Singapore   Sydney   Toronto

1 2 3 4 5 6 7 8 9   LCR   27 26 25 24 23 22

ISBN        978-1-264-28635-5
MHID        1-264-28635-X

e-ISBN      978-1-264-28636-2
e-MHID      1-264-28636-8

**Library of Congress Cataloging-in-Publication Data**

Names: Brady, Susan (Susan MacKenty), author. | Foutty, Janet, author. | Wooten, Lynn Perry, author.
Title: Arrive and thrive : 7 impactful practices for women navigating leadership / Susan MacKenty Brady, Janet Foutty, and Lynn Perry Wooten.
Description: 1 Edition. | New York : McGraw Hill, 2022. | Includes bibliographical references and index.
Identifiers: LCCN 2021058370 (print) | LCCN 2021058371 (ebook) | ISBN 9781264286355 (hardback) | ISBN 9781264286362 (ebook)
Subjects: LCSH: Women executives. | Leadership in women. | Leadership—Psychological aspects. | Career development.
Classification: LCC HD6054.3 .B7293 2022 (print) | LCC HD6054.3 (ebook) | DDC 658.4/09—dc23/eng/20220127
LC record available at https://lccn.loc.gov/2021058370
LC ebook record available at https://lccn.loc.gov/2021058371

*We dedicate this book to all women and allies
who are navigating their leadership journey.*

*To Jennifer and Julie for your unwavering
support, encouragement, and sisterhood while
I navigated every practice in this book.*

**—Susan**

*To the so very many who have positively
impacted my career, and to those whose impact
will benefit the next generation of leaders.*

**—Janet**

*To my parents, husband, children, and the communities
who empowered my leadership journey.*

**—Lynn**

# CONTENTS

# FOREWORD

We need more books like this by women leaders. Let me tell you why.

While career women face a multitude of challenges on the way up the corporate ladder, we are seeing steady progress. Women now hold many critical jobs overseeing some of the most important parts of the US economy. In 2021, the number of women CEOs on the Fortune 500 hit an all-time record: 41. And for the first time, two Black women are on the list. The numbers are better for the chief information officer (CIO) role—17 percent of Fortune 500 CIOs are women.

But as we all know, women's rise is also inconsistent and slow. The number of female CEOs is still just 8.1 percent of the total. The turnover among CIOs means it's tough to rise above that 17 percent. And the pandemic underscored the instability of all working women's lives, putting almost 5 million out of work, and by extension, shrinking the pipeline of future female leaders. What we clearly have seen is that without more structural, cultural, and personal support, the risk is that women will always be one economic crisis away from unemployment, underemployment, or career stagnation.

To really break through as women leaders, we need to hear from each other, learn from each other, and keep supporting each other. That's why books like this are so important. These 7

*Impactful Practices,* brought to you by authors Janet Foutty, Lynn Perry Wooten, and Susan MacKenty Brady, resonate with me. It's not just fancy theory or rhetoric—it's all based on real experiences.

In a quarter century at PepsiCo, including 12 years as chairman and CEO, I was also a wife and mother raising two daughters. My commitments and responsibilities for one of the world's leading food and beverage companies spilled into the needs of my family, and a lot of the time, I felt it was easier to invest in everything and everyone else first, essentially never getting to myself. My reality: being a CEO was brutal, exhilarating, gratifying, and immensely public, which often tested my resilience, authenticity, confidence, competence, and courage. I can confidently say the themes explored in this book, when viewed all together, wield immense power in helping anyone thrive in a leadership position.

First, *fostering resilience.* You'll need a lot of it. You're not just keeping up with pace and intensity—you will have more headwind than tailwind. You'll face some people hoping you don't succeed. Learn the layer of resilience that's needed daily so you will overcome setbacks and emerge stronger than before.

The way you *inspire a bold vision* is to go "outside in" as opposed to "inside out." If you say your bold vision is what the organization can deliver, that's inside out—but that may not be what the world requires. To really inspire a bold vision, you've got to have the courage to think outside in and 10 years out and back. For communicating and persuading people to buy into your vision, you need to *cultivate courage* because visions do not manifest overnight.

The practice of *embracing authenticity*—bringing your whole self to work—connects with the practices of *creating a healthy team environment* and *leading inclusively* to ensure that people follow you and foster team dynamics that lead to long-term retention.

How do you work with people? How do you build a team where people lead from their best self and don't put down other people? How do you call them out? How long do you work with someone before seeing they will not change, and retiring them? There are unconscious biased actions against not just women. Add race and it amplifies issues.

As women leaders, it's on all of us to pay it forward to the next generation. We must pass on everything that we learn in our positions of influence—as CEOs, and as women in the world, or as mothers, wives, and daughters. But that's not where it ends. Men, too, can benefit from what we've learned and experienced at the helm of our institutions.

Whatever *your* background or story is, you belong here. I'm glad that you've arrived. You owe it to yourself to thrive, but the world needs your contributions and will greatly benefit, too.

**Indra Nooyi**
former Chairman and CEO, PepsiCo

# ACKNOWLEDGMENTS

As with any book, this one came to be as a result of the support, courage, and brilliance of so many. The entire Arrive and Thrive™ Project was inspired by the legacy of the late Ellen Gabriel, who founded Deloitte's first women's initiative.

The Deloitte Ellen Gabriel Chair for Women in Leadership was established in 2005 by her Deloitte colleagues. The endowed fellowship is a tribute to Ellen's legacy and steadfast commitment to gender equity. Negotiation, gender, and leadership scholar Dr. Deborah M. Kolb was named as the first to hold the chair, followed by women on corporate boards expert Dr. Susan M. Vinnicombe, CBE, and mentoring expert, Dr. Stacy Blake-Beard. Susan MacKenty Brady was named to the chair by Simmons University President Helen Drinan and provost Katie Conboy in 2019.

## THE IDEA

With Ellen's legacy in mind, Helen and Susan pulled together a luncheon with Deloitte's Vice Chair of External Diversity, Equity, and Inclusion Terri Cooper, and Susan Esper, the Deloitte partner responsible for Simmons' initiatives. The four women spent the majority of the lunch chatting about their own experiences leading, when the idea of collaborating on a book for accomplished women leaders emerged. The idea felt like *kismet* and Ellen's spirit was undoubtedly with us that fateful day. It was Terri who instantly thought Janet Foutty would be a terrific coauthor for the project on the Deloitte side, and Helen Drinan in equal speed suggested that the incoming Simmons President Lynn Perry Wooten serve as a coauthor as well. This was how our "author trio" was born. The rest, as they say, is history. (Or, perhaps her-story.)

Susan, Janet, and Lynn got to work and identified the 7 Practices, shared their learning and lessons about each with one another, and engaged others to contribute insight, wisdom, and advice to the project.

# OUR THANKS

### Our brilliant editors:

Donya Dickerson of McGraw Hill, you believed in this project from the start and jumped at the chance to publish this book. Always as patient and kind as you are wise, thank you for guiding us to make even better what we have here for our readers. Candi Sue Cross, our "first editor" partner-in-crime, you continue to zero in on what matters most on the page and refine meaning with speed and grace.

### Our supportive teams:

We thank the entire Simmons University Institute for Inclusive Leadership team, The Simmons University Office of the President, including Chelsea Ginsberg and LaTanya Maxwell for their everyday leadership, and other members of the Simmons Community whose work, support, and energy impacted this book, especially Kathleen Rogers and Zick Rubin who leaped into all things contracting and led the legal aspects of the project on our behalf.

Laura Wareck and the Simmons Marketing Communications team for their magic with words, branding, visuals, and social media. Regina Pisa, partner and chairman emeritus of Goodwin Procter and board chair of Simmons University, for exemplifying visionary and authentic leadership.

Elisa van Dam for her expertise honing Practice 7, Annelle Rivera-Beckstrom for saving the day with speedy research turnarounds, Kristen Palson for leading permissions and the creative manifestation of all things Arrive and Thrive beyond this book, Kerry Brady Seitz for helping to hone and scrub the Values Exercise as well as the practices at the outset, Abby Bays for project management along the way, and Michele Houston, Tracie Charland, Gavin McGuire, and Art Corriveau who will take the goodness in this book and continue to make magic out of it.

Thank you to our colleagues at Deloitte, particularly Alicia DiGennaro and Donna Comerford for the myriad of contributions they made to bring every aspect of the book to meaningful life. We also thank Ashlyn Hoff, Jen Rood, and Rachel Orrison who were always at the ready to advise on research, marketing, design, and everything in between.

Thanks to Lynn's coauthors and collaborators, especially Dr. Erika James, Dr. Laura Morgan Roberts, Dr. Julie Ivy, Sonya Jacobs, Whitney Williams, Dr. Shannon Polk, Dr. Valerie Myers, and Dr. John Tropman who have been thought partners for inspiring research that makes a positive difference for the practice of leadership.

**Our inspiring contributors:**
For their invaluable perspectives, stories, and advice, we thank Gail Boudreaux, Dr. Albert Bourla, Anne Chow, Tiffany Dufu, Dr. Helen Drinan, Sandra Fenwick, Jen Fisher, Bill Flynn, Beth Ford, Carla Harris, Dr. Jim Harter, Dan Helfrich, Sally Helgesen, Linda Henry, Whitney Johnson, Natalie Martinez, Indra Nooyi, Jill Robinson, Dr. Richard Safeer, General Chuck Wald, and Amy Weaver.

## Our encouraging supporters:

In addition to all those previously mentioned, the authors also want to thank a few people who impacted this work and/or served as a support during its inception. Thank you to Margaret Alferi, Dr. Gary Bailey, Deborah Brittain, Dr. Sharron Credle, Sarah Cuthill, Jennifer Eckert, April Evans, Ann Fudge, Jenn Hernandez, Bill and Dagmara MacKenty, Mardee Moore, Suzie Murphy, Dr. Brian Norman, Kavitha Prabhakar, Lisa Rudgers, Tony Scoles, Darlene Slaughter, Paula Sneed, Lynn Tetrault, Estrella Traczik, Joe Ucuzoglu, and Tal Zlotnitsky.

# INTRODUCTION

## *Welcome Package*

*One must pass through the circumference of time before arriving at the center of opportunity.*

—Baltasar Gracián, Baroque writer and philosopher

You are leading, but are you *thriving*?

You have already "arrived" by all accounts. You *are* a leader. You *have* stepped in and stepped up. But there is more for you. An opportunity to intentionally thrive and create a greater impact for yourself and others. As you contemplate how much more you wish to invest of yourself to lead, it is time we talk about what it takes not just to arrive but also to thrive.

Are you getting the support required to thrive? Do you know how to ask for it? How do you thrive as a formidable leader while combating systemic barriers and unexpected challenges that add complexity? What is a realistic picture of leading for you that is framed by you and other leaders who are creating a new inclusive working world? How are you managing your best self and bringing out the best in others as you navigate the demands of life? What stories are you repeating in your head about who you "should be"?

If some of these questions leave you wondering, here is your first bit of wisdom to *arrive and thrive*: your thoughts and feelings are normal, and you are not alone. In fact, our hope is that as you read this book, you realize you are never alone. We are not meant to do much of anything alone, and through this book we want you to feel supported as you navigate from wherever you are. We know firsthand that as women rise into positions of greater responsibility and leadership, the risks associated with sounding, experiencing, or looking vulnerable become greater and greater. The "veneer of perfection" too often takes hold and robs women leaders of the ability to be real. Forced into being something or showing up as something women leaders think they should be (or are expected to be, given norms set mostly by men) keeps the cycle of "got to prove myself" or "not good enough" going. As a result, they feel there is little margin for error.

We authors have been in your shoes. We know you are not only curious, you are open to and wanting advice. You have the ideas, a drive to succeed, and the ability to empower others. The world needs you. A world with more successful, thriving women leaders is a better world for *all of* humankind.

The world also needs better, more diverse leadership, and the gender gap remains much too wide. Senior women in leadership deserve to thrive when they arrive, but hard-won practical and applicable wisdom from other leaders about the essential and most impactful practices that can help ensure success is needed. Women's leadership and decision-making have never been more urgent. The pandemic of the coronavirus (Covid-19) reared its submicroscopic head in December of 2019 and brought unprecedented consequences to the world in a span of six months, especially for women. An October 2020 Deloitte report, "Understanding the Pandemic's Impact on Working Women," found that nearly 7 out of 10 women who experienced negative shifts in their routine because of the pandemic believe their career progression will slow down.

We now know that a pandemic has the power to unravel our livelihoods, lifestyles, and turn our lives inside-out . . . swiftly. Seems ominous, we know, but it's not *all* bad news: a mass reset is happening. Pandemic-era realities have been intensified by the long-overdue awareness of the urgent need for racial justice and with it, total equity of opportunity for all citizens regardless of gender, race, ethnicity, ability, or sexual orientation. We have been learning and confronting fears, concerns, and cautions at warp speed—and facing them with courage.

In tandem, much attention is being paid to the creation of gender balance in leadership. The solutions—the programs, sponsors, and resources—that help women not only *arrive* at the top but *thrive* there will only increase, and for good reason: companies with gender-balanced leadership perform better. But how to do that effectively—how to make sure that women leaders succeed—is still an underexamined topic.

Navigating our leadership journey focuses on movement and requires intention and awareness and then agility-in-action. The practices in this book take you from learning to doing by guiding your movement as you intentionally arrive and thrive.

*Arrive and Thrive: 7 Impactful Practices for Women Navigating Leadership* ushers in critical and original advice for women facing disruptions that have little to no precedent. We knew it was time to boldly convey deep insights based on our own experiences and revelations. And we knew it could not wait.

Let us introduce ourselves.

Janet Foutty is executive chair of the board for Deloitte US, the largest professional services organization in the United States. She previously was the chair and CEO of Deloitte Consulting LLP. Janet is a frequent author and public speaker with executive-level audiences about the changing business landscape, leadership, corporate governance, crisis resiliency, equity, and technology disruption. Her thought leadership has appeared in business publications, including *Fortune, Forbes, Harvard Business Review,* and the *Wall Street Journal.* Janet is a passionate advocate for diversity, equity, and inclusion (DEI) in the workplace; women in technology; and the need for science, technology, engineering, and mathematics (STEM) education. She has founded Women in Technology groups in India and the United States.

A seasoned academic and an expert on organizational development and transformation, Lynn Perry Wooten, PhD, became the ninth president and first African American to lead Simmons University on July 1, 2020. Specializing in crisis leadership, diversity and inclusion, and positive leadership—organizational behavior that reveals and nurtures the highest level of human potential—Lynn is an innovative leader whose research has informed her work in the classroom and as an administrator. She first joined a university faculty in 1994 and has served in administrative roles since 2008. Lynn came to Simmons from Cornell University, where she was the David J. Nolan Dean and professor of management and organizations at the Dyson School of Applied Economics and Management. She also has had a robust clinical practice, providing leadership development, education, and training for a wide variety of institutions. Lynn is the author of two books and dozens of journal articles and book chapters.

A working mom of two teenage daughters, Susan MacKenty Brady's journey stems from a career in leader development with a focus on self-awareness and relational leadership. She has a "two-sided business card" professional identity: one as accomplished revenue driver and business leader; the other, leadership author and truth-telling humorist, and inspiring keynote speaker. Her insight is informed by 20 years of work in the fields of advancing women leaders and inclusive leadership, which has led to three previous highly acclaimed books. As the Deloitte Ellen Gabriel Chair for Women and Leadership at Simmons University and the CEO of the Simmons University Institute for Inclusive Leadership, Susan is committed to seeing equity in leadership in her lifetime. She believes the path to more peace and joy and less guilt and harshness *as well as* to better leadership is learning how to return to compassion (see Practice 1 for more on this!).

Simultaneously, our perspectives are backed by top-notch research and tools from our organizations, Deloitte and Simmons University.

Drawing on decades of our professional experience and our own personal insights, we want you to arrive and thrive. We have teamed up with and brought along well-recognized leaders who share their personal stories and insights exclusively and uniquely here to bring you the 7 Impactful Practices for Women Navigating Leadership:

- **Practice 1: Investing in Your Best Self.** Lead from the best part of yourself—and ensure you tend to your mind, body, and spirit for continual renewal.
- **Practice 2: Embracing Authenticity.** Bring your whole self to work with intention and ease.
- **Practice 3: Cultivating Courage.** Commit to action, alongside acknowledging and overcoming your fear of doing so.
- **Practice 4: Fostering Resilience.** Keep up with the pace and intensity while overcoming setbacks and emerging stronger than before.
- **Practice 5: Inspiring a Bold Vision.** Enroll others in a mission that awakens their spirit and desire to create a future that does not yet exist.
- **Practice 6: Creating a Healthy Team Environment.** Personify your organization's values and standards while creating an environment that is supportive, collaborative, and healthy.
- **Practice 7: Committing to the Work of the Inclusive Leader™.** Model the way for others while creating the culture of equity and inclusion needed for high performance.

We want you to see each practice as something you can come back to and work on over time, as you grow and as the context of your personal and professional life changes. Each practice offers a distillation of the best wisdom we could glean for you about every impactful practice, including wisdom from:

- Our own unique experience and learning
- The latest and most respected research and literature available
- Thought leader expert advice
- Leadership tips and stories from sitting or recently retired executives
- Tools for activation

Feeling supported wherever you are in this moment and in each milestone is critical as you evolve the 7 Impactful Practices. And you should know that others have tread similar territory in their positions of greater responsibility; they faced risk, turned adversity into opportunity, and led others through motivation and inspiration. That's why we felt it was conducive to bring in diverse outside voices with their own stories of impact, along with advice on the practices based on their own unique experiences.

- Gail Boudreaux, president and CEO, Anthem
- Albert Bourla, chairman and CEO, Pfizer, author of *Moonshot: Inside Pfizer's Nine-Month Race to Make the Impossible Possible*
- Anne Chow, CEO, AT&T Business, coauthor of *The Leader's Guide to Unconscious Bias*
- Helen Drinan, president emerita, Simmons University
- Tiffany Dufu, Founder and CEO, The Cru, author of *Drop the Ball: Achieving More by Doing Less*
- Sandra Fenwick, former CEO, Boston Children's Hospital
- Jen Fisher, chief well-being officer, Deloitte, coauthor of *Work Better Together*

- Bill Flynn, author of *Further, Faster: The Vital Few Steps to Take the Guesswork out of Growth*
- Beth Ford, president and CEO, Land O'Lakes Inc.
- Carla Harris, vice chairman, managing director, and senior client advisor, Morgan Stanley, author of *Expect to Win: 10 Proven Strategies for Thriving in the Workplace*
- Jim Harter, chief scientist, Gallup, coauthor *Wellbeing at Work: How to Build Resilient and Thriving Teams*
- Sally Helgesen, author of *How Women Rise*
- Dan Helfrich, chairman and CEO, Deloitte Consulting LLP
- Linda Henry, CEO, *The Boston Globe*
- Whitney Johnson, CEO, Disruption Advisors, author of *Disrupt Yourself: Master Relentless Change and Speed up Your Learning Curve*
- Natalie Martinez, CEO, Strong Women Strong Girls Inc.
- Indra Nooyi, former chairman and CEO, PepsiCo, author of *My Life in Full*
- Jill Robinson, CFO, Atlanta Braves
- Richard Safeer, MD, medical director of Employee Health, Wellness & Innovation, Johns Hopkins HealthCare
- Gen. Chuck Wald, president, Wald Strategy International, LLC
- Amy Weaver, president and CFO, Salesforce

Our contributors are proven leaders who bring industry and domain knowledge combined with the depth of leadership wisdom we know is necessary for getting it right.

Each practice presents a *self-awareness* and *self-practice* orientation, along with an *other-based* orientation, spanning individual application and broader team/culture application. Simply put, *Arrive and Thrive* is not the "next recipe for women's success" but rather offers fresh insights about the practices that, when not intentionally and continually implemented, lead to suboptimal impact, or worse, professional burnout. The paradigm for women for far too long has been about surviving—if you are lucky enough to arrive at the top. The 7 Impactful Practices for Women Navigating Leadership enable women to thrive and, in so doing, help others thrive as well.

As you rise into your position of greater responsibility, risk, and *reward*, this book offers the groundwork for making effective and fulfilling choices for yourself, your team, your industry, and even your community. Navigating senior leadership is hard enough for anyone in this complex world, and women face *even more challenges*. The gendered context we live in makes it harder for women to rise into positions of leadership, and we want you to feel a new level of support and practical wisdom as you navigate your journey from here.

Let's get started, shall we?

# INVESTING IN YOUR BEST SELF

*If you wish to be on a journey of significance, you'll need to invest in—and then lead from—your best self.*

   —Sandra Fenwick, former CEO, Boston Children's Hospital

## THE PRACTICE OFFERING

As a woman in a high-level leadership role, you've likely been assessing your environment and the people you lead, taking regular pulse checks to see if goals are being met and how your team has been performing. If you were to turn inward, however, and do a pulse check on yourself right now, who are you as (and are you functioning from) your best self? It's OK and common not to actually know! But it's imperative to understand your best self and intentionally lead from that place. If you don't, you run the risk of making negative impact you don't intend.

*Investing in your best self* encompasses leading and living your life from the optimum part of you. To invest in your best self requires getting to know yourself when you're at your best. This means exploring what your strengths and talents are, where you add value to others, what brings you joy and vitality, what well-being means for you, and understanding the self-care actions you need to take to truly thrive.

Figure 1.1 provides a visual of the connection of these elements to arrive at your best self.

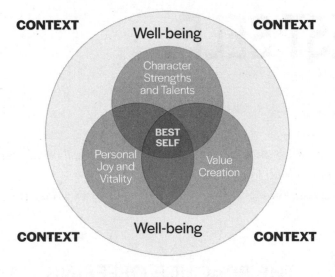

FIGURE 1.1 Best Self Connecting Points

Once you know you at your best, the job at hand is to learn how to consciously, and with intention, return to your best self over and over. Implicit in this notion is that it is impractical to think you will be able to lead your life from your best self *every moment* of *every day*. Life happens. You are human. Feelings arise. You react or get triggered. Disappointments ensue. You change or outgrow relationships or jobs, or they might outgrow you. Life shoves you out of your best self sometimes without warning, so you need to hone the practice of a "loving return" to these best parts of you and, ideally, as quickly as possible. Returning to your best self is a moment-to-moment practice. Nourishing your well-being will also change form and entail different self-care actions as you grow and change physically, professionally, mentally, emotionally, and spiritually.

Once you know you at your best and how to intentionally return to this place, you are ready to honor your own growth by updating your best self as you live out your life. Investing in your best self means revisiting *you* on a regular basis. These visits welcome increasingly deeper engagement and curiosity about your very existence in the present. How is your personal and professional growth changing you? What are you learning about your interests? What brings you joy? How might experiencing your own well-being be changing? How are you expending your energy in ways that deplete or invigorate you?

In honing the name of this specific practice, we asked dozens of women (and a few men, too!) what word they would use to replace "best." Not only did the words they used inspire a word cloud of desirable places from which to live life internally; it became very clear that each of us has our own unique view of what it means to be at our best. Here is what we heard: best self is . . .

FIGURE 1.2 Best Self Is

If you lead from your best self, you feel excellence and even elation within you. You can be present in the moment (or bring yourself back there in an instant), your not-so-constructive inner voices are quiet, you are your own exuberant cheerleader, and there is a narrow gap between your intention and your impact on others. Your replay of your words and actions makes you proud. You have listened well, and those around you feel heard and understood. You influence without unintended negative impact, and if you don't land as intended, you clean it up like clockwork. You know your strengths and value yourself. You care for your body, mind, and spirit. You are nourished by loving relationships.

As best self, you are, in other words, able to manage your energy and self-care, break the cycle of "not good enough," cultivate personal and professional boundaries, and return to this best self with intention when you get knocked off balance. You know when you have interacted with someone who leads from their best self because you feel better about you and inspired by them, as a result of the encounter. They not only leave no "muck" behind; they leave you feeling seen.

If this all sounds impossible at first blush, you may be coming from a place of perfection or status quo. Remember the "loving return." It isn't about doing it all perfectly; it's about being able to return to a place of caring for self and then (and *only* then) tapping your best to give to others.

Living your life from your best self is a win-win: it feels good to you and feels good to others, too. We asked 30 women who participated in the Simmons University Institute for Inclusive Leadership flagship program, *Strategic Leadership for Women*®, how they feel when they are leading from their best self. (Note: They spent concentrated time better understanding what best self personally meant before we asked this.) Figure 1.3 is their vivacious word cloud:

**FIGURE 1.3** Program Participants' Best Selves

We asked the same women what it felt like when their best self was blocked. Figure 1.4 is the resulting word cloud.

**FIGURE 1.4** Program Participants' Being Blocked

Who wouldn't prefer to feel the way these women did when they were at their best? Who wouldn't want to avoid experiencing all of those troubling, defeating feelings and thoughts that were brought on when their best self was blocked? If you want more of what it feels like to lead your life from your best self, it's time to learn how to *invest* in it. Like all of the practices in this book, investing in your best self takes conscious cultivation. We're going to guide you every step of the way.

## WHY THE PRACTICE IS ESSENTIAL

Deciding to invest in your best self means demonstrating compassion for all of *you*, and then caring for this best you like your life depends on it. Like it or not, this is a job of understanding, kindness, and self-respect. Self-love is regard for your own well-being and happiness. There are no shortage of books and studies that declare anything from 3 to 30 kinds of self-love. Let's boil this down to three key ways to love yourself: *physical*—refers to how you see yourself, *mental*—refers to how you think of yourself (self-acceptance), and *psychological*—refers to how you treat yourself (self-respect).

For your best self to manifest, you must make yourself a priority. And the good news about why best self requires self-love is that loving yourself might be the greatest revolution of all time. The more you love yourself, the more you will seek to be leading from your best self and the less nonsense you'll tolerate. If you put yourself at the top of your to-do list every single day, what would that mean for you?

Clinical psychologist and director of research and education for the Glendon Association, Lisa Firestone, PhD, asserts that there are well-documented consequences for not maintaining a healthy serving of regard for ourselves and engaging in self-compassion and self-care. These range from total energy depletion, resentment, and disengagement from others to getting lost in our critical inner voice, impairing our performance, and spawning a level of stress that takes a toll on our mental and physical well-being. In sum, Dr. Firestone says:

> . . . sometimes the messaging we receive to be giving of ourselves, to push ourselves to the limit, be productive, and forgo our needs can be taken to an extreme in our everyday lives. If we're not attuned to who we are and what we want, we can start to make sacrifices that don't just hurt or limit us, but actually negatively impact those we care for.

The argument for investing in your best self could begin and end with pointing out how much better you will feel when you lead your life from your best self. In actuality, however, the benefits extend to others, too. If you want to make a dent in the world, you'll need others to join you in whatever work you lead. The more you are leading from the best part of you, the more you will attract—and retain—followers.

## CULTIVATING THE PRACTICE

Ask any executive coach or leadership development consultant how best to understand your strengths, and most will likely suggest you engage in some self-awareness activities and reflections. Whether you choose the 360/multirater or self-assessment route, there is no shortage of tools you can use to illuminate the best you. Having said this, we have our favorites. In our corporate education leader development work through our Simmons University Institute for Inclusive Leadership, we use the Reflected Best Self Exercise™ (RBSE).

RBSE is a personal development tool that helps you see who you are at your best, engaging you to live and work from this powerful place daily. Created from research at the Center for Positive Organizations (Ross School of Business, University of Michigan), the RBSE has helped thousands of executives, managers, employees, and students discover new potential. Unlike most other feedback tools, the RBSE isn't limited to self-assessment. It invites people from your life and work to share stories of moments they feel they've seen you at your best, surfacing what few of us become aware of otherwise. The RBSE enables you to gain insight into how your unique talents have positively impacted others and gives you the opportunity to further leverage your strengths at work and in life.

Dr. Laura Morgan Roberts, a fellow of the Simmons University Institute for Inclusive Leadership, helped create the RBSE with her colleagues at the Center for Positive Organizations. Dr. Roberts defines strengths as the "qualities and capabilities that we possess that enable us to consistently produce desired results." She and her colleagues from the Center have found that it is vital for leaders to deeply understand these aspects of themselves. "Our greatest strength comes from the power within—it's about how we see ourselves as capable, resourceful, and caring. That's what affects our ability to adapt, rebound, connect, persist, and convert substantial challenges into opportunities for growing stronger," she says in the *Positive Identities* video series for the Center for Positive Organizations.

To discover and leverage strengths, the RBSE focuses on recalling high-performance episodes to characterize strengths in action and benchmark personal practices. In other words, leverage your strengths, and those of people you manage constructively, find situations that fit those strengths, and cocreate situations that engage those strengths. Strengths can emerge from talents, competencies, principles, and identities. Often, strengths are overlooked when, in fact, we should focus on honing them in a way that allows us to consistently perform at high levels.

So why focus on strengths over weaknesses? Which do you think will help you most in the long run in becoming extraordinary?

If your child comes home with a report card with four A's and a C, what is your typical response? We tend to focus on the C versus the A's. Parents around the world think the lowest grade deserves the most attention. This focus on deficiencies is also reflected in our approach to feedback and development at work. In the conventional view of development, we create a list of competencies based on observable indicators of success. Then we measure the performance gaps between requisite and demonstrated competencies, and focus on reducing those performance gaps by correcting deficiencies. The conventional view of development assumes that overcoming weaknesses will lead to excellence and that being well-rounded is important.

The RBSE and other strengths-based tools are exceptional because they help you *leverage* your strengths. Results can reveal a profound picture of flourishing versus getting by. According to Gallup, people who use their strengths every day are more likely to be engaged, and teams that focus on their strengths are 12.5 percent more productive. Yet less than 20 percent of global respondents use their strengths every day.

Advocating the "science of strengths" and the "practice of well-being," Values in Action (VIA) is another one-of-a-kind strengths-based assessment tool, which was created by the VIA Institute on Character. Designed by 55 scientists, the tool assesses 24 character strengths categorized into six virtues: wisdom, courage, humanity, justice, temperance, and transcendence. The VIA Character Strengths Survey is a scientific instrument measuring your strengths, and it's widely used in academic, corporate, and other settings. The tool focuses on a collection of positive individual character traits that are linked to your life satisfaction, well-being, and development. They are your key capabilities, influencing how you think, act, and feel and represent what you value in yourself and others. The scientific team contends that strengths correlate with the ability to flourish. Upon completing the survey, you receive an in-depth, one-of-a-kind report. When it comes to understanding your own strengths (and those of others), knowledge is power!

For the Simmons University flagship course, *Strategic Leadership for Women*®, RBSE is embedded in the course because it is a holistic process of gathering qualitative contribution stories for thematic analysis of best-self features and practices. Research indicates that people who receive best-self feedback have more personal agency, are able to better develop their resources, and have higher rates of well-being. The RBSE process is correlated with job satisfaction, intent to stay with one's job, and authenticity.

As we illustrate and celebrate *self* in this chapter, know that there are obstacles to a strengths-based approach to assessment. We've been socialized to believe in gap analysis, so strengths-based assessments feel countercultural and self-centered. We tend to seek and value deficit-oriented feedback. And let's be honest: high-quality, appreciative feedback is rare. Others don't give it and we don't seek it. Strengths-based development focuses on unleashing human resources by extracting and distilling a core set of qualities and strengths, and by identifying and leveraging strengths that are underutilized.

Strengths-based development builds off of research showing that while people remember criticism, they respond to praise, and that each person's greatest room for growth is in the areas of their unique strengths. The RBSE's distinguishing features are important. It asks for examples of your best, not "the" best. It asks you to solicit feedback from multiple groups both inside and outside of work through stories, not checklists—meaning what you do and how you do it. It seeks to uncover added value. It focuses on strengths, not weaknesses. It decouples evaluation and development.

While the official RBSE is best if facilitated and organized by a certified coach or facilitator, you can do a bit of this work right now. Dr. Roberts suggests you reflect on two types of high-performance episodes and then write down stories for each. First, write a story describing a time when you motivated someone else to achieve a high-performance episode. Then write a detailed story about when you were at your best and functioning in a high-performance way. Thinking of stories like this helps get you moving in the right direction on all things strengths and can lead you to moments when you were at your best.

# THE POWER OF
# KNOWING STRENGTHS

Investing in your best self starts in your heart and mind because if you are not aware of your best self or how to return there, you may be dead on arrival. You can't connect with the people you need to. You can't enroll them as a leader in where you want them to go. Most people would prefer to be in the company of others who are transparent, respectful, authentic, curious, assume positive intent, are able to give positive and constructive feedback, are patient, are able to listen carefully, and are able to show up as learners not knowers. It's critical to know the times when you feel you are at your best; you're doing many of these things. Here's the challenge: none of this is possible if you aren't aware of and actively managing your thoughts and feelings and ensuring your actions (what you say and do) are coming from when you're at your best. In essence, you need to know your strengths to (1) keep them moderate and (2) return to them.

### The Strength of Positivity: Susan's Personal Account
I get excitable and enthusiastic. I'm positive. Optimistic. I like to see a bright horizon around the corner at every turn. Sometimes

that leaves very necessary acknowledgements of hard moments unacknowledged by me. Where there is light, there is shadow. The light for me is that, on any given day, I might be found saying or doing something that might inspire others. The shadow is I might be found glossing over a more intense, difficult situation because I want to return to that happier or better place. That's been my own journey.

What I know for sure after over a decade of being a student, teacher, and author of this work is that if you want to find more ease in relationships, be more joyful, less critical or reactive, less stressed, more productive, move through conflict with more ease, or just plain be happier, then investing in your best self is essential.

Why do I know this for sure? I spent the better part of my early years (teens, twenties, even a good bit of my thirties) fairly unaware. I was smart and tenacious and had a lot of positive energy. That seemed to carry me far. At the same time, I was pretty brutal to myself. Despite what many would call a confident demeanor and a good track record of professional success, I had all sorts of reasons why I wasn't quite good enough. In my late thirties and early forties this critical, often harsh inner dialogue turned toward others more and more. I found myself annoyed with others whom I didn't think understood how to do something, or frankly, I just thought I could do several things better than others. Needless to say, both thinking I wasn't good enough and being critical (mostly only in my head) of others wasn't a winning strategy. And then I learned a few things about myself and how to manage me at my best that changed my life.

Here's what's in it for you. You can have more ease and joy in your life, less stress, and more healthy and productive relationships. Join me in getting to know and then returning to the core of your best self. This doesn't happen by accident. You need to cultivate it with intention.

Since the publication of Susan's last book in 2018, *Mastering Your Inner Critic*, she has thought further about things that get in the way of a leader's ability to lead from their best self. She knows that equity and inclusion—such a relevant and important charter for many organizations—require psychological safety. Now, given the working constraints and opportunity the pandemic has created, fostering an environment of inclusion is essential. An environment of belonging can't be fostered unless we understand what the unique strengths of each individual are. Belonging can't be fostered if we stand in harsh judgment of ourselves and others. While harshness is but one thief of being our best self, it certainly isn't the only thief.

Understanding how to draw the right boundaries (how to navigate with others in a way that feels right to others and OK for us) is also tricky territory. You probably feel this in your own life, asking questions like: How much information should I share about myself? How much should I inquire about another? When does inquiry feel intrusive? When does oversharing feel too much? The quick answer is that every person and every situation provides a different set of circumstances for what is acceptable and appreciated. The choices we make must be thoughtful for the context in which we find ourselves. The global health crisis and the entrenched issues of racial disparity we find ourselves navigating have brought this all to the forefront.

For you to be effective as a leader in your life, arriving and thriving, the best advice Susan has is to get curious about (and be gentle with) *you*. When have you felt you are at your best? When have you felt you weren't at your best? The invitation to you is to begin to think about what was true for you in both scenarios. Why? There isn't much better work for you to be doing than the work of cultivating your best self and then intentionally leading your life from there as often as possible. Your time to get started is *now*!

## AUTHORS' PICKS:
### Our Favorite Tools and Best Advice for Investing in Your Best Self

### Lynn Loves CliftonStrengths®

One of the instruments that have made the biggest impact not just on me personally, but also as I lead others, is the Gallup CliftonStrengths Assessment, an online measure of personal talent that identifies areas where an individual's greatest potential for building strengths exists. It measures your natural patterns of thinking, feeling, and behaving, and categorizes them into the 34 CliftonStrengths themes. Strengths are viewed as the result of maximized talents. The themes can be broken into four leadership domains: Executing, Influencing, Relationship Building, and Strategic Thinking. (See Figure 6.1 "The Four Domains of Leadership Strrength.") This framework lets you identify your leadership strengths and puts you in a reflective mode to uncover your best self. As we have spelled out in this chapter, our experiences lead me to believe that you will excel and become the absolute best version of yourself when you incorporate a strengths-based approach to every aspect of your life. Do more of what you do best, thrive, and increase your own well-being. You will be more engaged, productive, energized, and empowered to accomplish the most important goals you have set out for yourself.

The benefit of strengths work for me is that it enables me to identify my superpowers and use those superpowers as an energy source to lead. Knowing my strengths allows me to be intentional about using them and leaves me feeling I have a suite of resources inside myself that will help me in any situation. My top five strengths are Focus, Maximizer, Input, Learner, and Strategic. I tend to use my strength of Maximizer a lot! Whenever I confront a problem or opportunity, I think about the results we need to create and what excellence will look like if we are successful. From there, I reverse-engineer. This is my Maximizer at work. My Maximizer uses excellence as my measure and I want to take something from good to *superb*. I rarely settle for mediocrity and always push others to excel and be their very best self.

With the strength of Input, I'm collecting data and information. What do I need to understand to make a decision? I feel most productive when I have all the relevant information to make an informed decision. I crave data and the need to know more, which allows me to ask important questions to help us move forward in a thoughtful data-driven way. Using my strengths purposefully has given me a source of internal power to be more reflective of my leadership journey (there is a shadow side to every strength!). As I self-reflect, it is important to ask what is potentially getting in my way. Is this a blind spot for me? My goal is to use these CliftonStrengths themes in a productive way that will ensure others around me see it as a help, rather than a hindrance. In doing so, it has provided me with clarity about the leadership gift I want to share with the world.

## Janet Loves Business Chemistry

A tool that has been integral to how I build and lead teams is called Business Chemistry®. Deloitte created this system based on extensive research and analytics, plus years of proven success in the field. It provides a simple yet powerful way to identify meaningful differences between people's working styles to tap into the right mix of diverse work styles and perspectives. What I love about it is that it is tailored to the workplace and is a blend of personal introspection mixed with practical applications to more effectively lead others and get the most of your teams.

The framework is grounded in four primary work styles and related strategies for accomplishing shared goals:

- **Pioneers** value possibilities and they spark energy and imagination in their teams. They believe risks are worth taking and that it's fine to go with your gut. Their focus is big picture. They're drawn to bold new ideas and creative approaches.

- **Guardians** value stability, and they bring order and rigor. They're pragmatic, and they hesitate to embrace risk. Data and facts are baseline requirements for them and details matter. Guardians think it makes sense to learn from the past.
- **Drivers** value challenge and generate momentum. Getting results and winning count most. Drivers tend to view issues as black and white and tackle problems head on, armed with logic and data.
- **Integrators** value connection and draw teams together. Relationships and responsibility to the group are paramount. Integrators tend to believe that most things are relative. They're diplomatic and focused on consensus.

My work styles in order of dominance are: Pioneer, Integrator, Driver, Guardian. I have used this with many clients and my own leadership team for many years, and have also recently used this with my board so each of us can understand our respective chemistry. With all the topics and discussions that are in front of the board today, it is so important to understand how each member approaches topics and how they prefer to engage, especially in an increasingly virtual world. I want to create balance because all styles are critical for success. Where I may be focused on the big picture as a Pioneer, I need Guardians that bring the order and rigor. As a leader, you succeed if your team succeeds. Therefore, my goal is to always activate the potential benefits of diversity on my teams and optimize collaboration. Otherwise, I run the risk of some of the best ideas going unheard or unrealized, and performance could suffer. Business Chemistry is a great grounding mechanism to achieve those goals.

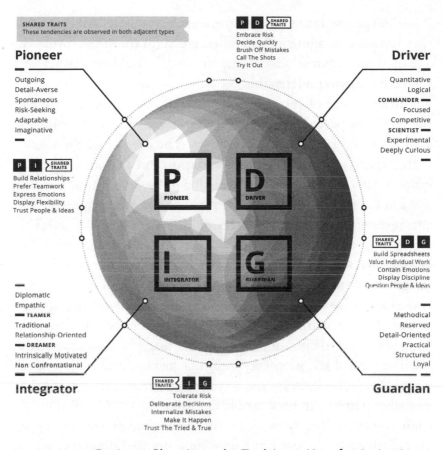

**FIGURE 1.5** Business Chemistry, the Tool Janet Uses for Activating Her Best Self and Optimizing Team Collaboration

© 2018 Deloitte Touche Tohmatsu Limited

## Susan Loves Myers-Briggs Type Indicator® and Enneagram

Two instruments have had the biggest impact on my own self-discovery over the years. The first, the Myers-Briggs Type Indicator® (MBTI), was introduced to me while I was an undergraduate student studying leadership at the McDonough Center for Leadership & Business at Marietta College. Widely used today in organizational life and leadership development experiences (over

2 million people take the instrument each year), the MBTI is both widely valued and researched. What it did for me at the formative age of 18 was offer self-awareness in a way I could remember and leverage my own preferences.

The purpose of the MBTI personality inventory is to make the theory of psychological types described by C. G. Jung understandable and useful in people's lives. The essence of the theory is that much seemingly random variation in behavior is actually quite orderly and consistent, being due to basic differences in the ways individuals prefer to use their perception and judgment. The vast research and simplicity of the tool allows one view of our preferences. In developing the MBTI instrument, the aim of Isabel Briggs Myers and her mother, Katharine Briggs, was to make the insights of type theory accessible to individuals and groups. They addressed the two related goals in the development and application of the MBTI instrument: the identification of basic preferences of each of the four dichotomies specified or implicit in Jung's theory.

The second self-discovery tool that has had the most impact on my life is the Enneagram, a system of personality typing that describes patterns in how people interpret the world and manage their emotions. The Enneagram describes nine personality types and maps each of these types on a nine-pointed diagram, which helps illustrate how the types relate to one another. It is common to find a little of yourself in all nine of the types, although one of them should stand out as being closest to yourself. This is your *basic personality type.*

The Enneagram Institute explains the tool as follows:

> Everyone emerges from childhood with one of the nine types dominating their personality, with inborn temperament and other pre-natal factors being the main determinants of our type. This is one area where most all of the major Enneagram authors agree—we are born with a dominant type. Subsequently, this inborn orientation

largely determines the ways in which we learn to adapt to our early childhood environment. It also seems to lead to certain unconscious orientations toward our parental figures, but why this is so, we still do not know. In any case, by the time children are four or five years old, their consciousness has developed sufficiently to have a separate sense of self. Although their identity is still very fluid, at this age, children begin to establish themselves and find ways of fitting into the world on their own. Thus, the overall orientation of our personality reflects the totality of all childhood factors (including genetics) that influenced its development.

If you're looking for an accurate portrayal of your preferences and character traits, the Enneagram offers many interesting and illuminating dimensions. Today, and like the MBTI, there are no shortage of online iterations (some free) to assess yourself.

Both the MBTI and the Enneagram helped me begin to see a clearer me. This awareness left me not only more conscious of my own (previously unconscious) preferences and styles, but also those of others. The tools ignited in me a lifetime of curiosity about human differences in personality, style, and relationship and leadership impact.

# A WELL-BEING PRIMER

Well-being is an essential ingredient to fostering resilience. While the bulk of our well-being wisdom is shared in Chapter 4, it is important to note that it is nearly impossible to return to our best self if we are not also actively taking care of ourselves. Dr. Richard Safeer, chief medical director, employee health and well-being, Johns Hopkins Medicine, wants you to ask yourself: When am I in *flow*? The psychological state of flow, according to positive psychology, is the mental state of being absorbed, focused, and enjoying your current activity (be that work, physical activity, etc.) It is a positive emotional and yet productive present state.

"When one is well, one has found a satisfaction and level of fulfillment and state of ease," Dr. Safeer says. He also espouses that well-being is not limited to a state of good health. It is much more. He is quick to point out that well-being is not an action but, rather, a state of existence and lives on a continuum where the individual decides their own well-being journey. "While it is helpful to have dedicated time to attend to your own needs, you don't necessarily need to carve out time for well-being. You do need to identify opportunities to *practice* well-being. It isn't necessarily having to go to the gym. Well-being needs to be part of your day, all day."

Thriving is an advanced state of well-being. Someone could feel well yet hasn't achieved their full well-being potential, which includes growth and new experiences. At a higher state of well-being, you are comfortable, content, and happy at that moment. You are not judging yourself over your state of well-being. Dr. Safeer reminds us that judgement is not an attribute that is consistent with a higher state of well-being, and that levels of well-being fluctuate throughout the day and your lifetime.

## THRIVE WITH THE ART OF RETURNING TO BEST SELF

All this encouraging talk about investing in your well-being and best self needs a grand reality check. If a part of you has been thinking, *yeah, I get how nice it would be to live life when I feel my strengths meet my value to others, which meet what makes me joyful, and I'm all up on my well-being practices, but seriously? Life is stressful. People can suck and I can be a disappointment, so I doubt this notion of living life from our best self is actually all that realistic,* you are smart and ahead of the game! It isn't practical to believe we can be happy and at ease and in flow every moment of every day. However, we *can* be in our best-self flow more often than not, and we *can* return there. Learning the glorious art of returning to your best self is imperative.

Let's just assume we will get kicked out of our best self. When we get kicked out of our best self (our flow) into any number of less productive places, it's usually because something happened. For example, let's say you were recently promoted to a role that has profit-and-loss responsibility. Weeks into the new role, you realize there is a massive amount of complexity and so much is out of your control—and you are depending on so many people. If you don't remember and employ your strengths, this ignites your stress and kicks you out of your best-self flow because you want to control every last detail and are driven by a need to succeed. While the impetus was the job change, you are dealing with a daily dose of stress, not flow. Whatever the trigger, the occurrence kicks us out of our flow. What we think and feel drives what we say and do, so we need to push "pause" before taking too much action when we aren't coming from our best self.

It goes like this: when we are in flow, we have a feeling of whole, enough, complete. We are typically present and engaged. When something happens that triggers us, we need to pause before our negative inner dialogue sends us someplace suboptimal. Usually, this suboptimal inner narrative, fueled by harshness and rarely moderate (which can become an outer narrative and verbalized quickly if we aren't careful), tends to show up as one of two overarching stances:

1. We point our harshness at someone else and we become critical of them. ("He doesn't know this target market, so why would he say that?")
2. We point our harshness at ourselves and become self-critical. ("I'm a fool to think this will work." "Why did I say that? That was stupid of me.")

This reaction is normal. Especially when we are trying hard at something or feeling like we have put everything on the line for someone or a goal. When we dare greatly, the critics will come. Our own and others. Consequently, we must manage our own return to our best self swiftly before we become depleted, or worse, resigned or reactive. Our return (a return to the belief that we are fundamentally worthy and of value regardless of our achievement or what others think) is critical if we are to play big in the world. It will become the essential practice to investing in your best self.

This is a moment-to-moment practice.

It begins with noticing when something isn't quite right for you. Imagine getting triggered and having a thought or feeling that is harsh and critical about yourself or another. Now imagine noticing that harsh thought and literally catching it with your hand (in your mind) because it is a fear-based thought fueled by disgust or harshness. The "catch" is when we push pause and examine the thought or feeling.

- What's going on for me right now?
- Why didn't this feel good to me?
- What's at stake?
- Why am I . . . angry, frustrated, impatient, annoyed, scared, flummoxed, outraged . . . and allowing myself to think or say critical things about myself or another?

*This* is the *pause*.

The reason you must practice mindfulness (noticing) and then pause as quickly as possible (other than all of the consequences for you and your relationships if you don't) is because the best part of you just got hijacked by your own brain. These moments can turn into a lifetime of anger and fear-based psychological warfare, or these moments can turn into opportunities to practice compassion with self and others and ultimately leave you feeling at peace. War won't get you back to your best self. Love will. You are in the driver's seat.

If you are triggered, chances are you are experiencing some level of amygdala hijack. The amygdala is a collection of cells near the base of the brain. There are two, one in each hemisphere or side of the brain. This is where emotions are given meaning, remembered, and attached to associations and responses to them (emotional memories). The amygdala is considered to be part of the brain's limbic system. It's key to how you process strong emotions like fear and pleasure.

Early humans were exposed to the constant threat of being killed or injured by wild animals or other tribes. To improve the chances of survival, the fight-or-flight response evolved. It's an automatic response to physical danger that allows you to react quickly without thinking. When you feel threatened and afraid, the amygdala automatically activates the fight-or-flight response by sending out signals to release stress hormones that prepare your body to fight or run away.

This response is triggered by emotions like fear, anxiety, aggression, and anger. This fear, anxiety, aggression, and anger is fair game for full attack on you ("I shouldn't have said that," "I am such an idiot," "I should know better") or someone else ("She's an idiot," "He's supposed to take charge now and once again is a disappointment," "What a dumb thing to say").

Thankfully, neuroscientists have discovered we have a newer, rational, and more advanced brain system since our early human days. The frontal lobes are the two large areas at the front of your brain. They're part of the cerebral cortex, which is where decision-making, planning, and basically all your thinking happens. The frontal lobes let you process and think about your emotions. You can then manage these emotions and determine a logical response. Unlike the automatic response of the amygdala, the response to fear from your frontal lobes is consciously controlled by you. *Breaking news!* You possess the controls to change your thinking. This is the best news you can imagine when you just learned how amazing your best self is, and you have the motivation to live as much of your life as possible from your best self.

When you sense danger is present, your amygdala wants to automatically activate the fight-or-flight response. However, at the same time, your frontal lobes are processing the information to determine if danger really is present and the most logical response to it. When someone says something in a meeting that annoys you (because your inner critic says they are stupid or just factually wrong or maybe just the tone of their voice is like nails on a chalkboard), we can likely agree you are not in physical danger. Your brain understands this and sees the "threat" (in this case, another person saying something irritating) as mild or moderate.

Mild or moderate "threats" trigger the frontal lobes to override the amygdala, and you respond in the most rational, appropriate way. ("I know what her intent was when she said the comment, even if it came out a bit harsh.") However, you might mentally be distracted by unhelpful and harsh thinking for far longer than necessary—even when your frontal lobes did their job.

As an aside, when the threat is strong, the amygdala acts quickly. It may overpower the frontal lobes, automatically triggering the fight-or-flight response. The fight-or-flight response was appropriate for early humans because of threats of physical harm. Today, there are far fewer physical threats, but there are a lot of psychological threats caused by the pressures and stresses of modern life. When stress makes you feel strong anger, aggression, or fear, the fight-or-flight response is activated. It often results in a sudden, illogical, and irrational overreaction to the situation. You may even regret your reaction later. Said another way, your amygdala is there to save your life, but it could also be the thief of your best self . . . if you don't manage it.

Daniel Goleman called this overreaction to stress "amygdala hijack" in his book *Emotional Intelligence: Why It Can Matter More Than IQ*. It happens when a situation causes your amygdala to hijack control of your response to stress. The amygdala disables the frontal lobes and activates the fight-or-flight response. Without the frontal lobes, you can't think clearly, make rational decisions, or control your responses. Control has been hijacked by the amygdala. Goleman also popularized the concept of emotional intelligence (EI) and its use to help manage your emotions and guide your behavior and thinking. EI refers to recognizing, understanding, and managing your emotions and recognizing, understanding, and influencing those of other people.

Needless to say, when we have been triggered by psychological threats, we are catapulted out of our best self. As long as our frontal lobes won the battle with the amygdala, a swift return to a better self is possible. You can return to your best self with regular practice if you: (1) notice when you are triggered, (2) take a breath and "catch" the thoughts and feelings, pressing pause on the runaway train that is a reaction, (3) compassionately consider yourself and others, and (4) explore what's going on in this instance.

For some, compassionately considering yourself and others can be the hardest part. The guilt we shoulder of not living up to whatever self-expectation we have can be all-consuming. So you might wonder how to get compassionate. One way is to channel the person who was most compassionate to you in your lifetime; someone from whom you felt caring, acceptance, affirmation, and appreciation (a grandparent or an adoring aunt or maybe a great friend or supportive boss). What would that person say to you at a moment when you're feeling harshness toward yourself or another? It's likely something along the lines of "whoa . . . easy now . . . gentle . . . it's OK . . . you're OK . . . you're doing the best you can . . . they are doing the best they can . . ." It might have been the simple act of receiving a warm hug. Getting compassionate can also be helped by channeling gratitude. What about yourself do you feel proud of or good about, and even grateful to have been able to do? What about another is something you can feel grateful for?

## YOUR TOP TOOL FOR RETURNING TO YOUR BEST SELF: SUSAN'S BEST SELF CENTERING PRACTICE™

I developed the Best Self Centering Practice with my colleagues at the Simmons University Institute for Inclusive Leadership. It is a practice of mindfulness designed to help you live as many moments of your life from your best self as possible.

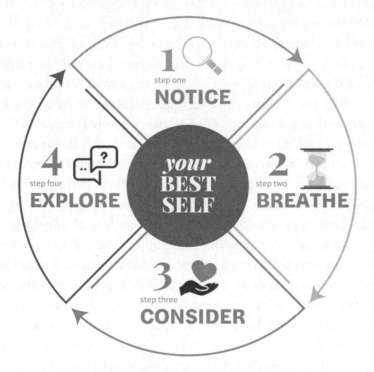

**FIGURE 1.6** Best Self Centering Practice

This is a four-step centering practice. If you put these steps into practice in the workplace and at home, you will get better results both personally and professionally—and you will live with more ease and joy.

## Step 1: Notice

It starts with noticing what you are thinking and how you are feeling. What is your internal narrative?

- What does it look like (visual)?
- What does it sound like?
- How does it make you feel?

You need to tune into what is happening in your mind. This is key to self-awareness. Instead of going through life on autopilot, you can become aware of what you are thinking and feeling. By noticing your narrative you take back your own power.

## Step 2: Breathe

This is easier said than done. Still, it is one of the most important things you can learn to do. Breathing actually counters the stress response. By taking a deep breath, you can slow things down. You get into trouble (internally and with others) when you react. When you get grounded you can learn to respond. This is an active part of self-management. Listening to meditations can help, but taking a time out for a conscious deep breath (or five) is meant for you to do in the moment and when you're triggered. Once you breathe in and out, think of something that makes you smile. Here's how it works: *breathe.* Think about something that makes you smile. *Breathe.*

Make a list of the things that make you smile. Maybe it's a picture, a special experience, or a special place. Capture what those things are. When you find yourself needing to breathe because you are triggered, if you think of something that makes you smile, you are essentially working *with* your limbic system to avoid an amygdala hijack and return to a calm center more quickly. When you smile, your brain releases tiny molecules called neuropeptides to help fight off stress. Then other neurotransmitters like dopamine, serotonin, and endorphins come into play, too. The endorphins act as a mild pain reliever, whereas the serotonin is an antidepressant.

In other words, smiling can trick your brain into believing you're happy, which can then spur actual feelings of happiness.

## Step 3: Consider

When we honor ourselves or others, we see them as whole and worthy as fellow human beings. We find something that we can appreciate about ourselves or the other person so that we can see us or them with a kinder, softer heart with compassion. Easier said than done in a moment when you are triggered. Here is where you start with the important job of compassionate consideration: you identify things you appreciate about yourself. The great news about discovering your best-self is that the job of identifying positive attributes about yourself shouldn't be that hard. What makes you special, unique, of value? What are three to five words that describe you at your best? Take time to identify what you appreciate about yourself. When you're triggered into feeling not good enough, lean on your awareness of your best-self attributes to bring you back to a place of self-compassion. When you are triggered into feeling something negative or harsh about another person, think about what they are like when they are at their best (despite not likely being at their best, according to your perception, when you have harsh feelings toward them).

## Step 4: Explore

Exploring is all about taking a minute to get curious. Asking yourself some questions about how you are feeling or what might be going on for the other person lets you better understand what is happening and then choose a different action. This is our destination.

The goal of returning to your best self is to realize and operate from a place where you see yourself (and others) as enough, whole, worthy, and complete. It's a return to respect for self and respect for others. It must be intentional, and it must be thoughtfully practiced. Self-awareness, which is what returning to your best self requires, is hard work, but it's essential to thriving.

## THRIVER'S WISDOM

### *Leading with Head and Heart: Sandra Fenwick*

One leader who is seen universally as someone who has many of the positive attributes and impact that come from investing in her best self is Sandra Fenwick, former CEO of Boston Children's Hospital. Sandra led a team of 20,000 people dedicated to improving and advancing child health through their life-changing work in clinical care, biomedical research, medical education, and community engagement. She retired in March of 2021. Here is her direct advice for navigating leadership as your best self on what she calls your "journey of significance."

### Learn to Be a Learner

Leading from your best self is about what you do and how you do it. The three C's are a great inner compass: curiosity, courage, and compassion. In my case, curiosity and courage are making things better for people and patients. Doing it with caring and kindness and thinking about people is where compassion is essential. Either working with people or on behalf of people, it returns to using your head and heart. What you do and how you do it.

Leading with compassion means caring about people, knowing them, their cares, awareness of human spirit, struggles, desires, their own goals. Then balancing the logic with the emotion. Thinking about how you can be a tough, hard businessperson but never forgetting the importance of the people you work with and the values that are part of those relationships.

Doing things that improve the lives of people is what I love. I'm not a doctor. I decided not to go to medical school. I'm not a scientist, a researcher, so I'm not discovering things.

But I've always wanted to be in health care and help others. So it's about doing it through others, enabling them to do their work, providing them with opportunities, supporting their work, supporting their development, providing them with the environment, the resources they need. That has been my reward and my personal return: watching and seeing what can be done through other people. That is why people are such a part of my journey of significance.

## Align Best Self with Strategic Priorities

I led a multidimensional turnaround at Boston Children's and one of my jobs was to set strategy for a broken organization. We had to determine how to survive and thrive as an independent children's hospital and one of the strong Harvard Medical School institutions. What needed to be done and in what order?

The first thing I did was ask, "What do we have to do immediately?" I wrote this down on a piece of paper that I still keep under my phone: fix the finances; build a culture of trust, respect, and transparency; align the physicians and get them on board with our vision; create a strategy; fix the broken infrastructure; and communicate, communicate, communicate. I then walked down this list which included creating a culture of being the best place to work. I picked six things I needed to do immediately and got started. They've always been there for me.

## Don't Go It Alone; Listen to Trusted Truth-Tellers

Surround yourself with one or a couple of very trusted people who have your back, care about you, are loyal and dedicated to you as a person, but also are dedicated to the institution; they will tell you honestly how you are doing. Have somebody whom you trust explicitly; it could be a communications expert, general counsel, a physician, a board member.

When I've gotten into tough situations, I've leaned on all of them for different advice and perspective. It could be a piece of data, testing a different audience, gaining an unbiased opinion, and many other invaluable inputs.

### Remember Your Accolades

Women like to ignore positive feedback, but when you learn you've done a good job, you need to hear it so you know how others perceive your best self. Make that one of the practices and keep on doing it better. Ask for feedback, hear it holistically, and ask how to tweak it. Most of all: when you hear you did a good job, remember that you did! These are the best clues about you at your best.

## POWER RECAP Investing in Your Best Self

### Key Points About This Practice

- If you lead from your best self, you feel excellence and even elation within you.

- You can be present in the moment (or bring yourself back there in an instant).

- Your not-so-constructive inner voices will quiet down (at long last).

- Your replay of your words and actions will make you proud; in other words, the gap between your intention and your impact on others is narrowing.

- You are listening with renewed intention, and those around you feel heard and understood.

- You influence without unintended negative impact, and if you don't land as intended, you know how to clean it up like clockwork.

- You know your strengths and value yourself.

## Suggested Actions

- Start with a self-assessment tool, such as the Reflected Best Self Exercise, Values in Action, CliftonStrengths, Business Chemistry, Myers-Briggs Type Indicator®, or Enneagram to start focusing on your strengths.

- Pay attention to when you are in flow.

- Define what self-care means to you and identify a routine.

- For returning, activate the Best Self Centering Practice (notice, breathe, consider, explore).

- Remember your inner compass of curiosity, courage, and compassion.

# EMBRACING AUTHENTICITY

*By definition, your authenticity is your competitive advantage.*
*Nobody can be you the way that you can be you.*
  —Carla Harris, Vice Chair, Managing Director and
    Senior Client Advisor, Morgan Stanley

## OFTEN OR ALWAYS?
## SHOWING UP AS GENUINE YOU

You may have heard authenticity is a necessary trait for leadership effectiveness. Current trends would say that without it, our growth and impact are significantly limited. On the surface, it might seem that a consensus exists about the meaning of authenticity; there is indeed widespread agreement that authenticity refers to that which is "real," "genuine," or "true." Below the surface, however, there is much less agreement, so you might find yourself confused about what natural characteristics and behaviors you should put forth. Depending on which social science they represent, researchers and scholars define authenticity differently and the definitions range greatly. In marketing and brand management, authenticity has become such an everyday term that it is used to describe products and services ranging from food and drink to artistic expression. But when it comes to us as individuals, and how we choose to express our own authenticity, those definitions are more directional than actionable; it is up to each of us to define our own version of authentic being, in general and in the workplace. Being our authentic self doesn't mean we eschew filters and boundaries in our self-expression. It means we approach any challenge or opportunity from our *best and most transparent self.*

So how do you want to *embrace authenticity*?

In Practice 1, we led you into the *arrive and thrive* arena with best self, which in itself may imply that you are ready to be your genuine authentic best self. However, there is a lot to consider regarding the significance and application of authenticity in the real world, *your* real world, every day. Especially as the Covid-19 pandemic forced most of us to pivot dramatically from a physical to virtual presence and, in turn, impacted how we show up and the expectations around that. We held critical meetings both large and small, conducted individual check-ins, and even onboarded new employees—perhaps with backdrops splashed with children's toys, lounging or disruptive pets, and sanitized packages freshly delivered. For many, these times were bonding; for others, they were awkward and uncomfortable.

In offering practical, lived perspectives and the freshest and most innovative thinking on the topic, our invitation to you is to think more intentionally about embracing authenticity in any environment. Let us explain:

Over the course of your career, you may have thought about authenticity and wondered: If the job I can never fail at is being myself, why does it seem to be a struggle sometimes? The seemingly simple advice to "be your authentic self" has many leaders confused. Is vulnerability really required if you wish to be real and, if so, how might that impact professional credibility? In a world where gender and other biases still often (thankfully not always) prevail, how can women be themselves, and what happens when they aren't?

## WHAT YOU BRING OF YOURSELF MATTERS

If, like us, you agree with the fabulous and inspiring Carla Harris, vice chair, managing director, and senior client advisor at Morgan Stanley, your authenticity *is* your "competitive advantage. Nobody can be you the way that you can be you."

Gail Boudreaux, president and CEO of Anthem, has some salient advice on this topic. She says,

> Speak out and do things that you truly believe in, that are tied to your value base, and you have to stay true to it. *You can't have a PR agent define that for you.* Certainly, people can help you frame issues, but this is not something you can delegate to others. It's immediately noticeable. One of the areas people point to or not. They know if you are authentic. You have to speak with your own voice and how you come across. The year of 2020 is a great example. As difficult and as transformational as that year was, it didn't teach leadership—it highlighted it. It allowed individuals to rise based on natural instinct and what drives us that makes us who we are.

No matter where you stand on the authenticity spectrum, it's safe to say that authenticity with people you know well is one thing. Authenticity on a broader platform is something very different. In essence, developing the confidence to be yourself in a big, visible job, openly sharing what matters to you personally and professionally, may be a real breakthrough for your leadership impact. We concur with Gail: authenticity matters.

Your goal as we go deeper into this practice of embracing authenticity is to discover your own depth and breadth of what makes you the *real you* in how you show up every day. Inevitably, your discovery and application will enable you to bring out your best self and inspire others to be their best self, too.

It's not a revelation: there are many leaders who progress in organizational leadership who are not authentic. They may be concerned with looking good and thus comfortable adopting a persona that's not really them. You likely know leaders who behave in this and other ways who simply can't build trust with others inside their organization. They leave a wake behind them and often can do real damage. Former CEO and chairman of Medtronic and author of the bestselling book *True North,* Bill George says: "If you want to be effective as a leader, then you must be an authentic leader. If you are not authentic, the best people won't want to work with you, and they won't give you their best work."

## AUTHENTICITY AND CHANGING TIMES: JANET'S PERSONAL ACCOUNT

The conversation today around "bringing your authentic self to work" is much broader than what it was when I started my career.

When I "grew up," the term *authenticity* was not a word used in conversation at all. Far from it. The expectation was that you were bringing your "work self" to work, not necessarily your "whole self." In recent years, the art of being authentic has become very front and center. And as I reflect honestly about my behavior, I've always been my authentic self, but I wasn't necessarily *trying* to be. Let me explain: I didn't grow up in a business environment, so I didn't know how to be anything but *me*. Said differently, I have had the privilege to lead in a way that wasn't overly worried about fitting a perfect norm or deliberately conforming to one. One way this showed up is how I connected with my teams. Instead of "happy hours," I was more inclined to organize "healthy hours" at the local gym or out for a walk. Instead of entertaining my teams over a round of golf and lunch at the club, I would host BBQs at my house with my young children present. I was being myself, and as a result, inadvertently shifting some norms.

I didn't know how to do anything different, in large part, because I didn't look, walk, or talk like many of my colleagues. In fact, when I was promoted to CEO, I got a lot of really wonderful congratulatory emails that I saved in a folder in case I ever needed cheering up—and one I obsessed over because it seemed a little backhanded. It congratulated me for "doing it my way." I kept wondering: What did he mean by that? How else was I supposed to do it? But eventually, I realized he meant I was successful not in spite of the way I led, but because of it. Perhaps the delta between what was considered "the norm" and me was so distant that it made it that much more natural to be me. That being said, I did quickly come to understand where some of the lines were, where some of the challenges lay, and how important it is, especially for women, to be thoughtful about embracing authenticity.

Both men and women have to remain sensitive to levels of professionalism as it relates to authenticity in the workplace. We have seen women less comfortable being authentic, and less willing to share the things they have grappled with personally and professionally. This has been true for us at times in our careers as well. Take the role of nurturer. We as women may inherently possess this trait, but it can also be expected of us, not just at home, but at work too—yet not valued as contributing to "real work." As a result, we tend to overcompensate in other ways, which could lead to moments of inauthenticity. The willingness to share of ourselves in contextually appropriate and honest ways is so important for building followership and building the next generation of leaders. In a survey Deloitte conducted on "covering"—a term coined in 1963 to describe how individuals with identities that are known to be stigmatized made a great effort to keep the stigma from looming large—countless respondents noted the impact that authenticity from an organization's top levels could have on their own openness and honesty. As one respondent put it, "Leaders have to uncover first. If they don't, we won't." As former chairman and CEO of PepsiCo Indra Nooyi shared with us, "It takes more effort to be inauthentic than it does to be authentic. If you are authentic, you are just one persona. If you're not, in every meeting, you're thinking 'what percentage do I show this time?' Why bother? Just forget it. Be yourself."

My own experience is that I evolved into broader leadership roles and found myself leading and working with people spread across multiple cities that I didn't know personally. As a response, I demonstrated an overabundance of formality in the manner in which I communicated and didn't talk about myself personally. This was true until I experienced a humorous, unintended breakthrough years ago that still has impact today.

One of my team members was at my house videotaping a holiday message to be shared with the broader practice. My husband and I had just built a DIY ice-skating rink in our backyard so family, including my kids who were eight at the time, could skate and play hockey. As such, my colleague said with great enthusiasm, "You need to share this!" I inherited his enthusiasm when he snapped a bunch of pictures. How could it hurt? Even though the backyard rink was in the "family" category of topics, it was light and sublime (perhaps code for can't be misinterpreted or stamped "weakness"). In those days, I had a strategy of writing and sharing "three-minute" messages with my team and encouraged other leaders to do the same with their teams.

That week, I opened my message with the skating rink narrative and picture to create intimacy with this large group of people. I painted the picture of kids skating in the backyard and how that created a very different family dynamic. We as parents appreciated our children's enthusiasm for Chicago winters; they appreciated us as parents for pursuing such an out-of-the-box experience. It was quite analogous to what we as a team were trying to achieve with our client. It was so easy, so noncontroversial, and to this day, people ask me about my skating rink and remember that message with such clarity. It made me human. It made me connected to something familiar. And when we get to know each other on a personal level better, it can make for higher-performing teams because you are more invested in each other to enable better collaboration and teamwork. It still makes me smile to this day because not only did this feel-good story stick; it brings back wonderful personal memories.

Another example a bit later on my leadership journey is what I like to call "the most important meeting I ever missed." At the time, my organization was in the middle of a significant acquisition that later would become core to our digital practice. We were to show up and bring our best selves to the soon-to-be-acquired agency offices on the West Coast. When I informed one of my leaders on the project that I was going to call in instead, let's just say this colleague was not exactly thrilled with me. But that meeting happened to be the same day as my twins' first day of high school. And every year since kindergarten, we've taken first day of school pictures on our porch. Did my twins care whether I was home to take their picture? They would never say that they did. But I did. And when I was done, I got on the call and told them exactly why I was 30 minutes late and still in Chicago. My team had it under control, the deal went through, and I got my picture. Two years later, I found myself at dinner with the leaders of that company. They told me that coming from a small, creative agency they were really nervous about joining "the suits" at our large organization. And they loved that I skipped the meeting. And the reason why? By choosing to spend that time with my family, it sent a strong signal to them that the organization they were joining is a place that encourages its people to be true to themselves and their values.

Imagine yourself as that effective leader who everyone wants to work with. Imagine embracing authenticity with intention and ease and bringing your whole self to work. What might be afforded to you? How might your performance improve? What would be possible for those around you? How can *you be you* and, at the same time, mitigate the perceived and real professional risks associated with embracing authenticity?

## WHAT DOES EMBRACING AUTHENTICITY MEAN?

At the 2021 Simmons Leadership Conference, 6,725 registrants received a survey about the importance of authenticity in the workplace. Susan and Lynn and their colleagues at the Simmons University Institute for Inclusive Leadership wanted to know what people think authenticity really means and what its impact is on individuals and organizations. The survey respondents helped clarify the top 10 qualities and behaviors for being authentic at work, helping bring sharper meaning to the definition.

A key finding from this research is that people define authenticity in the workplace in terms of *ethical integrity*. Qualities such as honesty and behaviors such as owning mistakes were prioritized. Respondents were asked to think of someone in their life who is authentic, and then share the three qualities that make that person authentic. Respondents did not choose from prompts, but rather provided their own spontaneous list of words or phrases via open-ended questions.

- By a significant margin, **honesty** was cited as the topmost important personal quality defining an individual's authenticity.
- Arguably, **transparency** and **openness** are subsets of honesty, and combined, these three words (*honest, transparency*, and *openness*) represent 41 percent of all responses.

- **Confidence** was the next most cited quality of authenticity. Current narratives around women and confidence support this quality's connection to honesty and truthfulness: "If I am confident, people don't question who I am." "I don't doubt myself, I'm secure in who I am and that's how I show up." "There is no tension between who I am, how I feel, and how I show up. I am therefore, presenting myself with authenticity."

The preceding narratives are supported by other words that surfaced in the study's top 10 list of words that define authenticity, such as genuineness, trustworthiness, and integrity.

In addition to identifying qualities of authenticity, a set of behaviors gleaned from current literature and popular definitions of authenticity in the context of work were offered to respondents to rank in order of importance. The following behaviors of authenticity resulted as the top five.

1. When I make a mistake, I own it and try to make things better.
2. I try to ensure that my actions have a positive impact on others.
3. I strive to tell the truth even if the news is bad.
4. I am able to act according to my personal values.
5. Who I am (my identity) aligns with how I present myself at work.

Based on the findings, the team of researchers at Simmons offer this as a refreshed definition of *authenticity*:

---

**The quality of aligning words and actions with the best and most ethical version of oneself.**

---

# HOW TO EMBODY
# THE PRACTICE

Discovering your authentic self is an evolution. "The reality is that people learn—and change—who they are through experience. By trying out different leadership styles and behaviors, you grow more than you would through introspection alone," according to Dr. Herminia Ibarra.

Dr. Ibarra is the Cora Chaired Professor of Leadership and Learning and a professor of organizational behavior at INSEAD. She is the author of *Act Like a Leader, Think Like a Leader*, and numerous articles, including *Harvard Business Review's* "The Authenticity Paradox: Why Feeling Like a Fake Can Be a Sign of Growth." Dr. Ibarra's research demonstrates that the moments which most challenge your sense of self are those that teach you the most about leading effectively.

By giving yourself permission to accept that you are—as we all are—a work-in-progress, and evolving your professional identity through trial, error, and self-forgiveness, you can develop a personal style that feels right to you and suits your organization's changing needs. Dr. Ibarra warns us about viewing authenticity too rigidly or having an unwavering sense of self. "A too-rigid definition of authenticity can get in the way of effective leadership." She depicts three problematic views of authenticity:

1. **Being true to yourself:** We have many selves (depending on roles we play) and we transform and evolve with various experiences as we mature through life. She asks: "How can you be true to a future self that is still uncertain and unformed?"
2. **Maintaining strict coherence between what you feel and what you say or do:** If you disclose everything you think and feel, especially when you are unproven, you lose credibility and effectiveness as a leader.

3. **Making values-based choices:** "Values that were shaped on past experiences can lead you astray." Especially when you move into bigger roles, behaviors that worked in a different context (she uses "tight control over operating details" as an example) might produce authentic but misguided choices.

With the expansive notion that your authentic self will shift over time and as you step into new contexts, how do you discover your "true" self? In his book *True North*, Bill George affirms, "Because your circumstances, opportunity, and the world around you are always changing, you will never stop calibrating your compass."

George and his colleagues at Harvard Business School have diligently been researching and exploring how people develop their authentic leadership, establishing the True North compass that helps you zero in on five major areas of personal development as a leader that will aid you as you discover your authentic self. They are self-awareness, values and principles, motivations, support team, and the integrated life.

As you consider each of the areas of the compass, George suggests you ask yourself these fundamental questions:

- **Self-Awarenes:** What is my story? What are my strengths and developmental needs?
- **Values and Principles:** What are my most deeply held values? What principles guide my leadership?
- **Motivations:** What motivates me? How do I balance external and internal motivations?
- **Support Team:** Who are the people I can count on to guide and support me along the way?
- **Integrated Life:** How can I integrate all aspects of my life and find fulfillment?

In Practice 1, we offered a myriad of tools to help you explore you at your best. Much of this discovery is grounded in self-awareness about strengths and motivations for when you feel in service of others and experience vitality and joy. Here, for embracing authenticity, let's turn to a values-based exercise that is sure to awaken your authenticity cells.

# TAKE TIME TO HOME IN ON YOUR VALUES

There is no shortage of tools you can use that will help you home in on your core values and principles. Since the bulk of them offer a similar approach, we offer to you our own Arrive and Thrive Values Tool™.

### Step 1: Generate a List of Values
Without overthinking your selections, circle all the core values that resonate with you, and add as many more as you'd like in the margins. Your final list should and will be long (perhaps more than 15). See Figure 2.1 for a comprehensive list of values you can pull from.

### Step 2: Scrub Your Values
Review your list and think carefully about each value included. Does each one resonate with you as a *core value* or *core principle*? If not, cross it off the list. You may remove as few as none, or you may remove several. The goal of this step is to have a final list that encapsulates your *truest* core values and principles. As you do this, you will realize that some values have greater meaning or staying power for you than others.

### Step 3: Prioritize Your Values
Now that you have this comprehensive and complete list, it's time to look at how each value relates to the others. What is the right order for your list? The goal of this step is to create a prioritized list

| | | |
|---|---|---|
| Accountability | Excellence | Perfection |
| Accuracy | Excitement | Piety |
| Achievement | Expertise | Positivity |
| Adventurousness | Exploration | Practicality |
| Altruism | Expressiveness | Preparedness |
| Ambition | Fairness | Professionalism |
| Assertiveness | Faith | Prudence |
| Authenticity | Family-oriented | Quality-oriented |
| Balance | Fidelity | Reliability |
| Being the Best | Fitness | Resourcefulness |
| Belonging | Fluency | Restraint |
| Boldness | Focus | Results-oriented |
| Calmness | Freedom | Rigor |
| Carefulness | Fun | Security |
| Challenge | Generosity | Self-actualization |
| Cheerfulness | Goodness | Self-control |
| Clear-mindedness | Grace | Selflessness |
| Commitment | Growth | Self-reliance |
| Community | Happiness | Sensitivity |
| Compassion | Hard Work | Serenity |
| Competitiveness | Health | Service |
| Consistency | Helping Society | Shrewdness |
| Contentment | Holiness | Simplicity |
| Continuous Improvement | Honesty | Soundness |
| Contribution | Honor | Speed |
| Control | Humility | Spontaneity |
| Cooperation | Inclusion | Stability |
| Correctness | Independence | Strategic |
| Courtesy | Ingenuity | Strength |
| Creativity | Inner Harmony | Structure |
| Curiosity | Inquisitiveness | Success |
| Decisiveness | Insightfulness | Support |
| Democraticness | Intelligence | Teamwork |
| Dependability | Intellectual Status | Temperance |
| Determination | Intuition | Thankfulness |
| Devoutness | Joy | Thoroughness |
| Diligence | Justice | Thoughtfulness |
| Discipline | Leadership | Timeliness |
| Discretion | Legacy | Tolerance |
| Diversity | Love | Traditionalism |
| Dynamism | Loyalty | Trustworthiness |
| Economy | Making a Difference | Truth-seeking |
| Effectiveness | Mastery | Understanding |
| Efficiency | Merit | Uniqueness |
| Elegance | Obedience | Unity |
| Empathy | Openness | Usefulness |
| Enjoyment | Order | Vision |
| Enthusiasm | Originality | Vitality |
| Equality | Patriotism | |

**FIGURE 2.1** Values List

of *your* values and principles. While all of the values on this list are your core values, this step will help you clarify which ones *truly* guide *you* to feeling *in alignment* and *at your best*. This may take a few iterations, but start by grouping your values into three sections: *High, Medium, Low*. Review your list and move the values under the appropriate header: High (importance) to Low (importance). It's unlikely these groupings will be even.

Last, remove the group headers and make one long list with all the values in order. Review and adjust any that feel out of order. This is not easy and it's OK if you feel a few are "tied." Give yourself permission to break the tie in whatever way suits you. Whatever choices you make, it is OK. The critical part of this step is to really assess the appropriate weight of each value and what it means to you.

## Step 4: Self-Define with Your Values

Look closely at the top three to five values on your list. These are your nonnegotiable values, meaning these are most critical to who you are and what you are looking for in your personal and professional worlds. As such, they (combined with other key words you have identified) should be a part of how you define yourself, and embraced as a vital and honored part of your authentic identity.

## How to Use Your Clarity About Values

Especially as you rise into positions of greater influence, grounding yourself in your values and principles will be helpful as you build your reputation and make tough calls and seek to be consistent as you do. Write your top values down and have them visible or easily accessible. Discuss these values and why they are important to you with a trusted colleague, mentor, or friend. Share them with your team. Get fluent in the language of your values, so they move from unconscious beliefs to clear and intentional drivers. Last, and in keeping with the wise words of Dr. Ibarra, we recommend you revisit the Arrive and Thrive Values Tool™ annually, to honor your own shifting authentic self.

# AUTHENTICITY IN ACTION

The application of your authentic self happens *in action*. You'll be confronted by your humanity. Being fallible doesn't mean you aren't purposeful and intentional. Expect that discovering and embracing your authentic self will feel beautiful and smooth only to a point—until you find yourself confronted with any number of obstacles that may result in:

- Being unable to please everyone
- Causing conflict or disagreement with others
- Causing disappointment among someone or a group
- Taking a different view or decision knowing others won't approve or will harbor judgment
- Feelings of vulnerability, fear, and doubt

Said differently, discovering and embracing your authentic self is beautiful and smooth until you find yourself . . . in a leadership position. People want to be led by someone who is real rather than constantly polished, so knowing what to express as your sincere self is key as evidenced in Amy's story, which follows.

Salesforce is an organization that is known for taking a stand on societal issues. President and CFO Amy Weaver is an outspoken advocate that "corporations should champion more societal responsibilities." Known for her authentic leadership style, she credits her past experiences for helping her wade through the emotions and constraints that come with managing the complex relationships of the corporate world. Amy explains:

> I've always worked in situations almost my entire life where I was either the only woman or one of very few women. What I wish I had learned earlier was that I didn't need to change my style. Out of law school, I clerked for a year, then worked for the Hong Kong Legislature for a year and I joined a New York law firm based in Hong Kong, one of the only women.

I spent my first few years trying to be one of the guys and modeled their behavior. They were great, but they all had completely different styles than I have. It took me several years to realize I was never going to be mistaken for "one of the guys." I was pregnant part of the time. I had to figure out what worked for me without a role model and without simply mimicking what the men were doing.

There was a moment when it came to a head for me. I had gone back to the States and I was preparing for a really tough negotiation. A senior male colleague came in to help me prepare. He said, "This is what you need to do: march aggressively into that room, lay down the law, preferably using a few choice words, and whatever happens, do not be too nice." He repeated that three times. I heard him out, kind of rolled my eyes, and said, "I'm not going to handle it anything like that. When is the last time you sent me into a large negotiation or a meeting and I didn't get you exactly what you wanted?" He was totally stumped. What he had described would have worked for him, but that was not going to work for me to succeed. If I had marched into that room, smacked the table, and started cursing, everyone would have burst into laughter, and I would have felt ridiculous because it would have been so inauthentic. By that point in my career, I realized if I could go in and use my own skills, I was going to be able to navigate the situation successfully. And I did. It was a turning point in realizing the power of relying on making connections. That works for me. Knowing the topic inside out works. Having that confidence and authenticity has made all the difference to me in my career.

Amy's story is so inspiring . . . and authentic.

So how do you collect your badges of authenticity upon arrival? Thriving in this practice requires steps and milestones. Returning to your best self and our invitation in Practice 1 to seek compassion and respect for self and others will be needed as you embrace—in action—your authenticity. The stakes only get higher for the work of being real as you take on additional responsibility and more complex leadership assignments.

We've come to appreciate how valuable consistent preparation is and the rewards it has for those we lead. We each work at this daily.

## Consistency and Preparation: Your Keys to Authenticity in Action

If honesty is the most cited trait of authenticity in action, doing what you say you will do and being congruent and consistent is imperative. So, too, is being prepared. A big part of authenticity is consistency and showing up in a consistent manner in all of your interactions.

In fact, the phrase "how you do anything is how you do everything" is a leadership principle of Janet's, which she adopted over the last five years or so:

> I first heard it from a figure within the sports industry when talking about a particular baseball player, and his incredible consistency in his interactions, in practice, in the community, and playing major league baseball. It's essentially about holding yourself to a consistent level of intensity, clarity, and directness in how you interact with others whether you are being watched or not. Especially as you advance, it's important not to get disconnected from who you are and what you're good at, and get enamored by the title. Otherwise, you can be perceived as disingenuous and this will make it more difficult to have your team come along for the journey. But if you are courageously acting in accordance with best self, that consistency helps influence followership. The concept is one that has been a lifelong learning principle for myself, I had just never heard it described in such a succinct, powerful way.

So how you do anything is how you do everything. Commit to personal consistency as you repeatedly show up and interact with all others, and it will help you embrace your authenticity and demonstrate it. We have all been around people who put on different personas and behave differently in the various situations they are in.

Consider Marley. Marley was an up-and-coming superstar, a hardworking, tenacious, and smart young associate. When it came time for promotion, one person on the promotions committee pointed out that Marley didn't seem authentic. The example given was as follows: Marley had been seen behaving differently when interfacing with senior executives (respectful, warm, patient) compared to how she treated several people in administrative support roles (gruff, cool, demanding). Not only did she shoot herself in the foot with the support staff (it didn't take long for word to spread), Marley also missed the mark on (1) being respectful and (2) being consistent in her treatment of all people at the firm. The executive on the promotions committee did not witness this herself, but her administrative assistant asked for her advice on how to handle Marley.

An easy way to embrace authenticity and help others do it as well is to treat every human being with the same care, respect, professionalism, and engagement, regardless of role, title, status, or positional power. When leaders model this consistent treatment, others follow. When leaders stand up and confront inconsistencies in behavior like Marley's, it allows for the psychological safety needed for inclusive cultures to thrive. (More on this in Practices 6 and 7.)

Maybe a more complex, sophisticated example of consistency is how you prepare. Preparation is extremely important to who you are and how you lead—not to mention the fact that it exponentially builds confidence, as Amy alluded to. The idea here is that you need to prepare for a difficult conversation with a staff person with the same level of discipline and rigor that you would a client or a peer. When you consistently commit to the art of being prepared, you do two meaningful things: (1) show those who are in receipt of your preparation that you care, thus thumb-printing your brand as someone who is prepared, and (2) build trust that others will value your perspective because it is one that is thoughtful.

# BE THOUGHTFUL IN HOW YOU SHOW UP

Jill Robinson, CFO of the Atlanta Braves, shares how she learned the hard way about what it means to be authentic.

> Before I hit the VP level, I worked for a very charismatic person who embodied the notion of authenticity. What I didn't understand was that in many respects, he had earned the right to be fully himself. There was immense respect for the guy by most everyone who worked with him. My error was that I mistakenly believed that it was OK for me to be super casual and gregarious (my true nature) the way he was.
>
> I have come to believe that as you develop competence in your role, bringing in your personal attributes becomes OK. But it needs to be balanced and measured. It's OK to have a personality but not at the expense of your own professional credibility. For me, this meant not always leading with a joke. Recognizing not everyone has this style and not everyone will respond well to it. I had to learn to be more nuanced in my approach to how I show up while staying true to me. It's not about covering up; it's about being intentional about what you let out.
>
> Further, when you are the only woman at the table and everyone else is a man, that can be intimidating. So many women juggle two jobs: the one we are paid for and the one we manage at home that we aren't paid for. What's hard about being authentic for women is how much or how little

we convey the actuality of the "second shift" in our workplace conversations. My brain is never able to shut off one
job or another. My own personal style helps me bridge the
gap—because I talk smack with the guys. I never felt lacking in confidence to be me. It's just harder to break into a
conversation if I walk into a room with a bunch of men who
are talking about golf (a sport I don't play) than a bunch
of women.

## THE ADORNED ELEPHANT IN THE ROOM: EMBRACING YOUR AUTHENTIC LOOK

In a Coqual study of professionals about what it takes to get to
the next level, one aspect of the survey findings points to the con-
cerning fact that women are held to stricter standards in terms
of appearance yet denied feedback on what those standards are.
Writing for *Newsweek* about workplace dress codes troubling
women for decades, Emma Bell points out that women are scru-
tinized far more than men for what they wear, and high heels
epitomize the lose-lose nature of getting the dress code right, for
example.

> Stilettos are seen as an important symbol of power for
> women, a marker of high status, despite their impractical-
> ity and physical strain that they put on a woman's body.
> The fact that Hillary Clinton opted for "nearly flat shoes"
> was deemed worthy of comment. The treatment of former
> Australian prime minister, Julia Gillard, is another example
> of how unjust the scrutiny of women's dress can be to their
> professional image. As Gillard explained in her recent auto-
> biography, throughout her leadership her body shape and
> clothing were considered newsworthy in ways that did not
> apply to male counterparts. Cameras were trained on her

bottom; news reports focused on her choice of clothes; and an incident when she tripped in India was reported frame-by-frame in a front page spread of a leading Australian newspaper.

Let the gravity of that sink in—Julia Gillard was the twenty-seventh prime minister of Australia and the first and only woman to date to hold that role; 570 bills were passed by the Australian Senate under her leadership in three short years. But her choice of clothes was routinely a focal point?

Choosing how to dress has real implications and connection to showing up as a woman leader who embraces her authenticity. When it comes to appearance, do what makes you feel good. Women can feel pressure to look a certain way from head to toe. But what we advocate is to recognize your aesthetic superpower and go with it. If it's reading glasses with a bold frame, brighter lipstick on Fridays, or a statement jacket—be you. You don't have to check every arbitrary box of how a woman should show up, but stay cognizant of your professional environment and audience. Ask your small cohort of friends and trusted advisors for feedback. You can feel good in what you wear to work *and* thoughtful about the impact of your choices at the same time.

## DON'T LET "EXECUTIVE PRESENCE" DERAIL YOU

Over the years, we've had discussions with professional colleagues, both men and women, about physical presence at work—both in dress, but also polish and preparedness. From coaching managers about how to have effective feedback conversations (tricky any way you slice it, but especially if the feedback is coming from a man to a woman) to advising groups of women about how to have an effective physical brand, this topic isn't easy and needs to be addressed. Because like it or not, how women physically show up and what other people think of us *does* impact our confidence, competence, and performance.

Also, the gig can be rigged and not in favor of women. What we mean can be summed up in two words: executive presence. There have been many attempts to define what this means. In fact, what every study on the topic can agree on is that the definition is often mysterious, murky, and subject to vastly differing perspectives. Yet senior executives surveyed in one particular study say executive presence accounts for 26 percent of what it takes to get the next promotion.

Janet has seen this to be a classic issue that many professionals face, from a wide variety of backgrounds, when they're on deck to become partners. She was at that exact stage when she experienced it herself:

> Over the course of my career, I was told I needed to work on my executive presence. And more times than I can count, I've heard concerns about whether an individual "looks the part." Though there were a few exceptions, often there were no details behind that feedback. I'm all for taking constructive criticism seriously, but those kinds of comments are unproductive. Because they say more about our biases about who does and doesn't belong in the executive suite than they do about an individual's merits. That's why I have a rule for myself. If I'm going to offer someone advice about how to get to the next level, I have to make it both specific and actionable. No vague criticism that boils down to nothing more than "I just don't see you there." Instead, I have to help them understand exactly what they need to do to get there. And those on the receiving end of vague feedback should push back—ask for more specifics. Don't allow a nebulous phrase like "executive presence" without explanation to derail you.

# VULNERABILITY WON'T KILL YOU— SPEAK WITH COURAGE

In her book *Daring Greatly*, Brené Brown explains that *vulnerability* is the source of authenticity. "Vulnerability is uncertainty, risk, and emotional exposure. Shame is the fear of disconnection. Is there something about me that others might not find good enough? In order for connection to happen, we must allow ourselves to be seen."

The confluence of crises and complexities that emerged in 2020 has been an interesting test for leaders of their authenticity, and probably the biggest test that Janet has faced because of the blending of social and political issues into the professional environment at unprecedented levels. "Even though I have always lived with a strong set of values, I've not talked about them explicitly in a public setting as they relate to how I think about politics and how I think about society broadly. The care with which I've had to navigate that line is extraordinary right now, especially as a woman." It's getting better for sure, but there can be an unconscious bias about whether an issue is truly a critical business issue if it's brought up by a woman leader versus a man—even at the most senior levels after credibility has been built and proven. Women are considered more emotional so there may be assumptions that ". . . well, she's raising this point because she's leading with her emotions, but is this truly a major issue for our business?" As with any major business decision—have the data and evidence (or examples) to back it up, couple that with tangible near-term next steps on how to address it, and even preview it with a group of influential peers to adopt support.

We will explore the practice of instilling courage in-depth soon, but it would be shortsighted not to address the difficulties and complexity of speaking from your authentic self. As we all know from firsthand experience, having the courage to be authentic with people you don't know and that you might not ever get to meet is not easy.

Social media has given executive leaders many more platforms from which our voice and perspectives are heard—and that, of course, is a double-edged sword. In many ways, the risks have never been *higher*, because when a leader says something, they are now at the mercy of the reach and consequence of social media outlets.

It's a risk. But it shouldn't scare you. Using your authentic voice in the right way can be one of the most valuable ways to honor your authenticity *and* be effective as a leader. Speaking with courage begins with the leader. Role modeling this and being clear that it's not comfortable for you either can be galvanizing. It is your job to be transparent that you're not always comfortable being clear.

When we talk about being authentic, vulnerable, and transparent, that does not necessarily equate to "share everything." Setting boundaries is OK; we need to be thoughtful of what we share and when. Consider what's appropriate in the context of the moment and allow for some self-preservation. Do it if it will give you energy and/or help others. Janet shares:

> When I started talking about being a breast cancer survivor, which I did not do for five years after I had finished my treatments, the first few times, I said, "I'm talking about this for the first time and this is not something I like to talk about or even want to talk about, but it's important you know this about me." I was essentially trying to say: I know you think I have this perfect life, and this is my way of showing you that my life is complicated and messy just like yours. But most importantly, it may also give others the courage to speak up and not suffer in silence.

Next, in Practice 3, let's explore how courage can help us be our best self and embrace our authenticity.

# AUTHORS' PICK:
## Our Favorite Tools and Best Advice for Embracing Authenticity

### Susan Loves the Authentic Leadership Aha Exercise

I attended a weekend-long workshop with the coauthor of *Finding Your True North: A Personal Guide and Program to Discover Your Authentic Leadership,* Nick Craig. Nick had recently partnered with Bill George and was building out the Authentic Leadership Institute (now the Core Leadership Institute).

My favorite exercise during this experience was when we were put in groups of three and asked to reflect and then share three times in our professional life when we felt we were at our best. We were joyful. We were engaged. We were *on purpose.* Where were we? What exactly were we doing? Who were we with? What was special or different about this moment or experience?

It was in recalling these three experiences that I became clear about my true authentic self. What I valued, when I felt at my best, but especially when I felt the "real me" was *wanted.* The three experiences all had this in common: I embraced my authentic self, and the way I showed up (real, genuine, me) was not just accepted, but was celebrated.

## THRIVER'S WISDOM

### *The Real Deal: Carla Harris*

Carla Harris is widely known for her talks such as "Differentiate Yourself" and "Being Smart Isn't Enough." On top of her extensive career in arriving and thriving in banking and wealth management, she is also a proud bestselling author, TEDx speaker, and gospel singer. Here she is, the real Carla!

## Effective Leadership Requires Authenticity

If you can't be who you really are, it's very hard to inspire people to be their best selves. That is the issue. For people to outperform, they have to bring it. They have to bring all of them. If any piece is constrained, I believe it compromises productivity, the output, and creativity.

Leading authentically is absolutely critical. Leaders the world over have been tested in the last two years especially [in response to the Covid-19 pandemic]. I don't know a leader among us who wasn't tested by wondering how to lead in this moment. Anyone who had gotten to this position of leadership all of a sudden was being called upon, asked, required to bring their real self to the table. Many couldn't. They didn't know how. They didn't even ask the question: Who am I? All these years, putting on the face was something that was "required." That is what leaders before them had done. From high school to now being in this seat, they didn't even know where to start.

## Authenticity Allows Me to Be the Best Carla

In a client-facing business, the clients have to trust you, and when I'm taking a company public, they are trusting that I'm going to get this right. The only way that I could get them to trust me was by bringing the real Carla to the table. When they saw that, when they smelled that, they connected immediately. I was able to own the relationship in a way my colleagues weren't. In earlier days of my career, I struggled. What should I do? I saw this person being successful, so I thought I needed to do it the same way. None of that measured up. None of that led to really having a client talk to me honestly, trust me for my advice, seek me out for what qualifies me, until I brought the real Carla to the meeting.

I was told by a senior leader that I was smart and worked hard, but that I wasn't "tough enough for this business." My first reaction was, what is he smoking? You can call me a lot of things, but "ain't tough" ain't one of them. It was a wake-up call that the real Carla was no longer walking into Morgan Stanley. I saw myself as tough. Somewhere along the way, I had lost my voice, swallowed my voice, lost my confidence, and that girl was not the one showing up every day and being as successful. I went out of my way to underscore my toughness until my persona caught up with the perception. I went out of my way to walk tough, eat tough, drink tough. That is who I am, so be that Carla. Good, bad, or ugly.

By definition, your authenticity is your competitive advantage. Nobody can be you the way that you can be you. I can never out-Janet Janet. There might be some things that Janet does that I admire that I might want to have in my tool chest also. That's good, but I must own it in a way that is authentic to Carla. Don't try to be like Janet.

## Don't Be Seduced by the Trap

You start falling into the trap of trying to be like someone else, and that puts you behind the eight-ball. Anytime you're not bringing your authentic self into any kind of relationship—managing someone, colleagues, then you impair the potential trust of the person in that relationship. You could lose your edge. You could lose your client. You could compromise your leadership because those being led by you feel there is something not right or they're not getting the real you, so that is going to cause them to pull back a little bit on what they could offer. As a leader, you want everybody's

150 percent investment, not just the 100 percent. If you're about to step off the cliff, you theoretically want them to follow.

## Showing Vulnerability Is Simply Showing How You Feel

Ask, what is the risk in showing who you really are or how you really feel about something? What is the big deal about showing your vulnerability? Your vulnerability is your ignorance; "I have no clue, I have no idea." That may be showing some vulnerability. "I'm afraid of this virus." This is showing vulnerability.

I wish I would have had this resolve to be my authentic self earlier in my career. It is the thing that makes you powerful. I was less powerful trying to be something or someone else. In the late eighties, it was almost a requirement for women to wear charcoal gray, navy blue, brown, black suits. There was a spoken and unspoken conformity. Unspoken, you weren't supposed to bring your authentic self to that environment. There was a prescribed uniform that was a prescribed way of doing things. No big earrings and don't wear fingernail polish because they will just follow the colors when you use your hands while you are speaking. There was an implicit message not to be your authentic self if you were feminine, especially if you wanted to wear polish or have flowing hair. That decidedly went away in the mid-90s so there is no excuse for today's woman not to be her authentic self.

## Check in With Yourself Often

We evolve from every experience we have, not to mention everything that we learn changes us in some way. Before the pandemic, we were running so fast that I would argue most of us failed to check in and say Who am I today relative to who I was in 2012? Relative to 2019? Check in with yourself often, especially after you've had an adverse action. If something has not gone well, take some time to say: What happened? Why didn't I see that coming? What could I have done that would have prepared me? Did I react correctly? Just study the thing for a few minutes. It doesn't take a long time to determine whether or not you changed, what happened. And move on. That is how I stay authentic.

## POWER RECAP Embracing Authenticity

### Key Points About This Practice

- The willingness to share of yourself in contextually appropriate and honest ways is important for building followership and building the next generation of leaders.

- Authenticity is a competitive advantage.

- Honesty, transparency, and openness are top personal qualities that define your authenticity.

- As an authentic leader, if you make a mistake, own it, and try to make things better.

- Values shaped on past experiences may not fit the current situation.

- The application of your authentic self happens *in action.*

- Consistency and preparation are keys to your authenticity.

## Suggested Actions

- Use the Arrive & Thrive Values Tool and take time to home in on your values.

- Use the Authentic Leadership Aha exercise.

- Talk to an individual or group that initially makes you feel uncomfortable.

- Enlist a trusted support system for feedback on how authentically you are coming across.

- Prepare for a difficult conversation or meeting in a new way and see how it feels.

# CULTIVATING COURAGE

*Commitment to action is a commitment to understanding the
realities of what you may be learning about yourself. Courage
is about introspection: knowing yourself, growing yourself,
confronting your flaws, and admitting you don't know everything.*
—**Anne Chow, CEO, AT&T Business**

## COURAGEOUS THRIVING

In *The Six Signature Traits of Inclusive Leadership*, published by
Deloitte, courage is defined as:

---

**Putting personal interests aside to achieve what
needs to be done; acting on convictions and principles
even when it requires personal risk-taking.**

---

Beginning with self-advocacy, when we are on our advancement path, having courage upon arrival in leadership roles quickly
becomes a practice that impacts many others who depend on us to

lead the way. You may have been in a position where you've had to make a bold decision or have a difficult conversation, and in those moments, you likely had to abandon your comfort zone and use courage to get through. Courage is the willingness to act when it is hard, risky, or scary to do so. In the context of business strategy, it's the willingness to engage in courageous conversations and to make and execute courageous choices.

*Cultivating courage* allows you to take risks not in the absence of fear, but despite it. Eleanor Roosevelt said, "You gain strength, courage, and confidence by every experience in which you really stop to look fear in the face. You must do the thing which you think you cannot do." Fear is often perceived to be a negative emotion that holds people back from reaching their full career potential. The world makes us believe that fear is, at best, unprofessional and unproductive and, at its worst, it can be paralyzing and stall or derail one's career and development. However, fear is inevitable. There is no courage without fear.

Real impact does not manifest without making difficult decisions. As leaders, we must encourage our teams to do the things that scare them, just as we did, to achieve success—even if it means working a little harder or making mistakes. When you come to a point in your career where you look at your to-do list and know how to accomplish every single thing on it with ease, something has gone wrong. The things that terrify us most will often provide the greatest value down the road in terms of growth, innovation, transformation, and much more.

Instilling courage optimizes your impact and strategy, your team and your people. Courage at work is action-oriented and directed at moving the group toward better outcomes or embracing the personal risk inherent in practicing new behaviors to get better at capabilities. The report from *Deloitte Insights*, "Human Inside: How Capabilities Can Unleash Business Performance," emphasizes how unforeseen and unforeseeable problems and complications, as well as opportunities, require unexpected responses centered in the courage to manifest them. When an organization offers a training ground for solving problems with autonomy, new capabilities are bred and released to flourish. In this type of environment, "problems can intrigue and motivate—piquing our curiosity, capturing our imagination, demanding creativity, and creating urgency and commitment."

It's safe to say that courage—acting despite uncertainty or opposition—is sewn into the fabric of one who arrives and thrives. By no means does that signify courage is a constant, no matter how frequently or how long you have arrived and thrived. Over the course of our professional lifetime, while confronting different challenges with an array of consequences, we should not expect to be courageous at all times and in all circumstances. We continue to strengthen our muscles of courage as we live our lives and navigate complexity.

When courage is directed toward meaningful action, in service of achieving something rather than just directed at overcoming fear, it strengthens itself. If you are not able to possess and emit the courage to deliver the direct conversations with your people in how they're doing, and what they're focused on, the effects for you and your team are significant.

In a world with more uncertainty, people may feel real fear around the workplace, results, and performance, as well as about their own potential, future relevance, and identity; courage to act is more important than ever.

Anne Chow was named CEO of AT&T Business in September 2019, making her the first woman to hold that position, and the first woman of color CEO in AT&T history. She's responsible for 30,000-plus employees who collectively serve three million business customers worldwide. Besides her obvious level of influence and responsibility as a leader, Anne is a Juilliard-trained pianist. And she's not afraid to share her personal journey.

Where does my courage come from? A bunch of it comes from my origin story and that my parents were immigrants. They came with less than $500 to this country. They came not knowing the language. They came here in pursuit of the pro-verbial American dream. When I think about the risks they took to do that, my risk aperture is probably far greater than others who don't have something comparable in their back-ground. I have many lessons from my parents, one is this constant obligation in a good way to do good for others, with an underlying service to others always. When my parents came here, they had a sponsorship family. They could have never gotten to where they've gotten without the support of other people, so the sense of community is really important. My dad taught me that to be good, you have to do good. That is the foundation for my courage but as my career has progressed, I garner what fuels my courage from others for whom I'm working so hard to make a difference.

What motivates me, whether giving a keynote, partici-pating in a meeting, or writing a blog post, is the opportunity to build connection with people. And if I can reach just one person and help them on their journey, it is worth my time, investment, energy, and effort to do it. Each positive affirma-tion from a young leader, or an Asian American woman, or someone I have mentored and watched their success, some-body I have sponsored and seen them blossom, I garner energy and satisfaction from those outcomes. That's what fuels me. As a woman of color, a minority female senior exec, and there are not many, I have stood out. When I hit mid-dle management, I looked up and saw there are not a lot of people who look like me, I thought about it and got this huge surge of obligation to say, "You know what? Part of my job lies not in the climb itself nor to just fulfill my greatest potential. The most important part of realizing my greatest potential lies in what I can do for others.

What you can infer from Anne's story is that courage exercised for greatest impact to and for others often feels most worth it.

## HOW TO UPLEVEL YOUR COURAGE

One might wonder about the job of instilling courage when you're a woman. Do women have a greater need to be liked, thus making the job of being courageous even harder than for our male counterparts? Do women avoid courageous acts for fear of disappointing others? As it turns out, there isn't much evidence to prove this so. There is, however, widespread agreement that the need to be liked is a human need that would be true for all genders.

In Roger Covin's book fittingly titled *The Need to Be Liked*, the author, a registered clinical psychologist and researcher, professes that almost everyone has a fundamental *need* to be liked by other people. It is a healthy and normal part of life. (Conversely, there is infinite debate about the consequences of *wanting* to be liked—at least to the point of "overpleasing," which is unhealthy.) When it comes to risk aversion, however, the story for women is a bit more nuanced. Do we women have a greater fear of risk? There is no shortage of literature on gender differences in risk-taking. Studies featured in the *Journal of Economic Literature* and *Psychological Bulletin*, among others, have shown that, in general, women are slightly more risk-averse than men when it comes to economic, intellectual, and physical risks. As some amount of risk-taking is critical for applying all 7 Practices, it's worth delineating that more recent studies show it depends on what the risks are:

- A study by the University of California–San Diego scholars found that gender differences in risk-taking behavior (RTB) are a little bit more nuanced. In RTB involving gambling, health, and recreation, women were found to be less risk-takers, but in taking social risks, there were not many gender differences. Also, in what they called "positive domain" or risks that involve large benefits for a fixed small cost, women were found to be more likely to engage in such risky behaviors. (Examples of positive domain risks include things like trying to sell a screenplay you have written to a Hollywood film studio, calling a radio station where the twelfth caller will win a month's worth of income, sending out 30 applications for high-paying jobs after graduating from college, regularly visiting a professor in her office hours and then asking her for a letter of recommendation.) Bottom line: the study found that women tend to take more risk than men when they expect good outcomes and greater positive consequences, and less severe negative consequences.

- A study by University of California–Santa Barbara and San Diego scholars claimed that they found "strong evidence" that women are more risk-averse than men when it comes to financial risk-taking.
- In the context of the global banking industry, a study found that female directors in the boardroom did not negatively affect performance and risk-taking. In fact, the study pointed to the *benefits* of gender diversity in the boardroom.

Citing her own research findings, Elaine M. Liu, associate professor at the University of Houston's Department of Economics, says, "Many studies find that women are more risk-averse than men. [My research] tells us that the gender gap in attitudes toward risk among children is influenced by culture and social environment. It may not be an inherited trait." So it may be that gendered aversions to risk will evolve as our own adult expectations (less gendered orientations) of children evolve. Until then, we can assume that the way girls are raised from an early age—even in modern society—invites eventual internal biases about "being careful." Taking risks might be something we encourage girls to do more.

In the meantime, we all still need to confront risks, and this will mean we need to cultivate the courage to do so.

As a leader, you will need to look at first the aspects of cultivating personal courage and then the aspects of cultivating a culture of courage. Risk will be unavoidable in both arenas, and one without the other will be suboptimal for arriving and thriving.

## CULTIVATING PERSONAL COURAGE

The word *courage* comes from a Latin root word meaning "of the heart." Dr. Brené Brown translates the word to "wholeheartedness." "Courage, when it first came into the English language," she explained in her now-famous TED Talk, "the original definition was, 'To tell the story of who you are with your whole heart.'"

The phrase "daring greatly" is from Theodore Roosevelt's speech "Citizenship in a Republic." The speech, sometimes referred to as "The Man in the Arena," was delivered at the Sorbonne in Paris, France, on April 23, 1910. According to Dr. Brown, this is the passage that made the speech famous:

> It's not the critic who counts; not the man who points out how the strong man stumbles or where the doer of deeds could have done them better. The credit belongs to the man who is actually in the arena, whose face is marred by dust and sweat and blood, who strives valiantly . . . who at best knows the triumph of high achievement and who at the worst, if he fails, at least fails while daring greatly.

Dr. Brown thinks the first thing we have to do is figure out what's keeping us out of the arena. What's the fear? Where and why do we want to be braver? Then she wants you to figure out how you are currently protecting yourself from vulnerability. What is your overprotective armor? Perfectionism? Intellectualizing? Cynicism? Numbing? Control? "It's not an easy walk into that arena, but it's where we come alive."

Cultivating personal courage requires you to acknowledge what you don't know, ask for help, and act despite risk of failure. All three actions are likely to invite feelings of discomfort and vulnerability. Let's dive into each of these and explore how they may work in your life.

## Acknowledge What You Don't Know

"The future belongs to the learners, not the knowers," said Richard Leider, founder of Inventure—The Purpose Company and preeminent life coach. Let's face it: the knowledge economy does not encourage people to admit when they lack knowledge or skills. However, by refusing to acknowledge that we don't know something, we limit our chances for personal improvement. Saying "I don't know," practicing intellectual humility, and adopting a growth mindset are necessary and require courage.

## The Wonders of Growth Mindset

Dr. Carol Dweck coined the terms *fixed mindset* and *growth mindset* to describe the underlying beliefs people have about learning and intelligence. Dweck found in her research that one of the most basic beliefs we carry about ourselves has to do with how we view and inhabit what we consider to be our personality. A "fixed mindset" assumes that our character, intelligence, and creative ability are static givens that we can't change in any meaningful way, and success is the affirmation of that inherent intelligence, an assessment of how those givens measure up against an equally fixed standard; striving for success and avoiding failure at all costs become a way of maintaining the sense of being smart or skilled.

A "growth mindset," on the other hand, thrives on challenge and sees failure not as evidence of unintelligence but as a heartening springboard for growth and for stretching our existing abilities. Out of one of these two mindsets, which we manifest from a very early age, springs a great deal of our behavior, our relationship with success and failure in both professional and personal contexts, and ultimately, our capacity for happiness.

Dr. Dweck found that at the heart of what makes growth mindset a winning proposition is that it creates a passion for learning rather than a hunger for approval. Despite a lack of research about women having an aversion to risk due to fears of disapproval, adopting a growth mindset is an effective strategy if and when people-pleasing thoughts arise. Adopting this mindset will not only decrease your worries of being discouraged by failure, but Dr. Dweck's research tells us you are unlikely to see yourself as failing in hard situations; you will see yourself as learning. Human qualities such as creativity and intelligence, and even love and connection, can be cultivated through effort and intentional practice.

Cultivation of a growth mindset will help you cultivate courage because it *rewards* not knowing it all. "I don't know" turns a lack of knowledge into an opportunity for personal improvement. You *currently* lack the knowledge or skills but you're willing to work to acquire them.

## Confirming Fears: Beware of Confirmation Bias

The risks of knowing and thus avoiding the need for courage to some degree are vast. When people refuse to admit what they don't know, confirmation bias (also known as certainty bias) comes into play. When you think you know, you deliberately seek out evidence that confirms your supposed knowledge, and avoid that which might show you that you don't know enough to make a rational decision. Confirmation bias is a phenomenon where decision makers have been shown to actively seek out and assign more weight to evidence that confirms their hypothesis, and ignore or underweight evidence that could disconfirm their hypothesis.

Studies have shown that once someone has formed an initial judgment or opinion about something, there is a strong tendency to reaffirm that assessment by intentionally seeking out evidence that will confirm or reinforce that point of view and to deny or intentionally avoid considering any evidence to the contrary. Once you have formed an opinion, you embrace information that confirms that view while ignoring or rejecting input that casts doubt on it.

Using meaningful examples from their marriage to underscore the "peril of confirmation bias," social workers Linda Bloom and Charlie Bloom write in *Psychology Today* that confirmation bias suggests a lack of perceiving circumstances objectively. You pick out those bits of data that make you feel good because they confirm your preconceived beliefs. When this happens, you become unable to reassess your perspective, and your assumptions become your hardcore truths.

For obvious reasons, letting confirmation bias run amok can be limiting and even dangerous. The danger is that when you don't gather or even remain open to accepting new information, even when doing so may help you update assumptions, your conclusions may no longer be accurate or valid. Confirmation bias often leads to the creation of self-fulfilling prophecies that occur when you act according to your closely held beliefs and expectations, and unknowingly create results that affirm those beliefs, thus reinforcing your prejudices.

In their cautionary tale against feeding a "closed loop of defensiveness and antagonism," which can negatively characterize any relationship, the Blooms state: "Being a permanent prisoner of confirmation bias involves the greatest loss of all: the loss of the freedom to make conscious, responsible choices for our own life based upon trustworthy, informed, and accurate information, rather than conditioned beliefs that may no longer be valid or relevant to our current reality."

## Learn to "Think Again"

*Think Again* author Dr. Adam Grant wants us to "embrace the joy of being wrong." He states, "Rethinking is a skill set, but also a mindset. We already have many of the mental tools we need.

We just have to remember to get them out of the shed and remove the rust." Would you believe that one of these tools is actually doubt? Dr. Grant surmises if we use doubt as a basis for embracing the unknown and being wrong, courage over comfort can prevail. His position is well-cemented by evidence showing that creative geniuses are not attached to one identity, but constantly willing to rethink their stances, and that leaders who admit they don't know something and seek critical feedback lead more productive and innovative teams. As a mindset and a skill set, rethinking can be taught, and learning to *rethink* may be the secret skill to give you the edge in a world changing faster than ever.

When it comes to cultivating courage, the opportunity to shift your apprehension from admitting you don't know (or have willingness to openly admit you could use more information than you currently have) could make all the difference. Admitting you don't know is truly the first step in cultivating courage, and it also takes courage. Lean on growth mindset, seeing the peril of confirmation bias, and the terrific work of Adam Grant and others who are calling for leaders to reward not knowing.

Acknowledging that you don't know gives others around you permission to do it, too. You might just jump-start a learning culture, which is necessary should courage be practiced at work. We'll address this in a bit.

## The Antidote to Fear: Ask for Help

Where do you stand in confronting the "Will you help me?" fear? If it's been cringeworthy in the past, know that both the language and your intentions behind the request can be exercised with a greater degree of ease when courage prevails. And simply put, there is no substitute for help toward how to proceed after admitting when we don't know something.

There are times to be a big bold leader, and there are times to be unafraid to say, "I don't know what to do," and "Help me think and talk through what we should do about this." Asking for help is when you channel your own growth mindset and seek help with the right actions to take. Margie Warrell, international speaker on courage and advocate for gender diversity in leadership, states, "As with so many things that would serve us (and others), our fear is what gets in the way. Fear of overstepping a friendship. Fear of appearing too needy. Fear of imposing. Fear of revealing our struggle and having people realize we don't have it all together after all."

If you struggle with asking for help, take heart that you are not alone. There is something in our human psyche that hates to admit it is hard to ask for help. Much of our reticence to ask for help points to worrying about what people think. Concern about being judged by others is a very real feeling. If you find it hard to ask for help, you might be thinking, *I should be able to handle this myself,* or *I'm unsure of where or to whom to go for help with this,* or *This isn't bad enough to ask for help,* or *What will X think of me if they know I need help?* Keep in mind that everyone in your life has had to ask for help with at least one area of their lives. As you contemplate asking for help, be sure to go back to the "flow" state of your best self, ground yourself in your strengths, and from that place of self-awareness and self-assuredness further invest in yourself. Asking for help means you care enough about yourself to increase the likelihood that things will work out in your favor by getting the support you need.

Garret Keizer, author of *Help: The Original Human Dilemma*, says, "There is a tendency to act as if asking for help is a deficiency. That is exacerbated if a business environment is highly competitive within as well as without. There is an understandable fear that if you let your guard down, you'll get hurt, or that this information [asking for help] will be used against you."

Social psychologist Heidi Grant, author of the book *Reinforcements: How to Get People to Help You*, has found that people grossly underestimate the odds that others will help them. She writes:

We're reluctant to ask for help in part because we feel like there will be a pretty good chance we'll be rejected. So, why do we think we're going to be rejected? It comes from a failure of perspective-taking. When I'm asking you for help, I'm focused on how effortful or unpleasant the request is, how busy the person is, how annoying it'll be for them to help me. All of that makes me think they're not going to say yes. What I'm not thinking about are the costs of saying no, and they really are quite high. Most human beings buy into the idea that good people are helpful, and so most people don't like to say no to a request for help.

In 2018, CivicScience polled over 2,000 US adults on their comfort with asking for help in a variety of different situations. Findings from the responses may have been provocative in some areas, but not surprising. Findings for thought:

- Individuals underestimate the likelihood that someone will help them by as much as 50 percent, meaning that people are far more willing to help than we may assume. To receive help, however, we have to ask.
- 41 percent do ask for help in the workplace. That leaves 59 percent who do not. Based on average stress levels, it seems that those who do ask for help at work are far more likely to be stressed out on a daily basis than those who do not. Although this may seem counterintuitive, this suggests that employees who are seeking assistance really may have more responsibilities than they can handle on their own. As a result, asking for help could be more of a necessity than a choice, to keep work projects moving forward.
- From the perspective of gender, those who do ask for help are split fifty-fifty. However, this study showed those who do not ask for help at work are slightly more likely to be women. In comparison, women make up 57 percent

of those who ask for help at home. This sharp contrast suggests that gender continues to play a major role in how individuals behave in public and private spheres, and further, where people feel most supported in speaking up.

M. Nora Klaver, whose book is *MayDay! Asking for Help in Times of Need*, says, "People often believe they don't have trouble asking for help, when they do. Sometimes they sit on projects for weeks because they didn't want to ask for help."

In Susan's book, *Mastering Your Inner Critic*, she encourages readers to flex their help-asking muscles in micro and macro ways. In fact, she's a staunch believer in modeling behavior she advocates. "I imperfectly practice what I preach. Today, if that means avoiding feeling disappointed in myself or someone else because I am aware enough and courageous enough to ask for what I want, then I am making progress. The journey starts with a moment-to-moment choice, and with recommitting to yourself each and every day. It's all about progress, not perfection." By this, what we want you to know is that when we ask for help, it doesn't reflect poorly on our ability; it simply conveys that we can't perfectly know how to do everything all the time and this is not only OK—it's critical to modeling the kind of learning that leaders need to live by.

## See the Ask as a Source of Strength

When you're faced with feelings or experiences that are challenging, frightening, or overwhelming, learning how to be selective when you reach out can also increase your chances of receiving a safe and compassionate response. In learning to discern, you will surely be tested like Janet was below. The most important lesson is viewing asking for help as a source of strength versus weakness, which will simultaneously help you identify the right people.

Early on in Janet's career, she had been offered a role for a client that she wasn't quite ready for:

I didn't have the courage to say, "I'm probably not ready for this." I did have the courage to surround myself with the right team that would make the situation as good as possible. But it still took a couple of months and getting pretty deep in a rather dark place before I summoned the courage to go ask for help within our organization way up the chain. We eventually lost the client for other reasons. But from a personal courage standpoint, the fact that even though late, I still raised my hand and asked for help was credited as a great success. And what was truly right for the situation. I've told this story in a lot of leadership settings, especially where I feel like teams keep things bottled in and don't ask for help.

## Act Despite Risk of Failure

When we make a personal act of courage, we speak up in some way, shape, or form despite the fear or risks of doing so. In other words, we have a courageous conversation. Courageous conversations mean being fearless in having direct conversations but in a thoughtful and gracious manner. At work and in organizational contexts, courageously acting despite risk of failure usually comes down to "speaking up."

As a young partner, Janet was confronted with a situation where her client was asking the team to do something they couldn't do.

I was not the closest to the situation at all, but I got "voluntold" to be the one to go tell the client what they didn't want to hear. I prepared like mad for that discussion and went in with the CEO of the client organization. The CEO was furious during the meeting when I started to explain why something couldn't be done and offered alternative solutions. By the end of the meeting, he was actually starting to listen. We left and the other partner who I had been with said, "That went well! You didn't need to sweat that much." The client called and said, "If you want to continue doing this work, here are the four things we need the team to do and here are the three things we will do." He did not say, "Janet, you were right," to be clear, but he did say, "We're going to do these four things and we'd like to continue working with you."

Janet uses this story as an example of the importance of preparing intensely to help mitigate the risks involved with having to tell someone what they do not want to hear, as well as having the courage of your convictions to act in a way that may be perceived as unpopular, but the right thing to do.

No stranger to risk taking, Anne Chow recommends:

When you are faced with a decision and you are worried about failing, think about two paths: think about the best thing that will happen if you move forward and play that out. The best: "Wow, I get the funding to help the firm drive the innovation to serve the market." Then, think about the worst thing that will happen if you move forward and play that out. The worst: "I don't advance my idea and therefore, I will never know." That is unacceptable. You have to get over the hurdle of asking. You advance the business case, and they say no. You are no worse off, but you learned. Why was it rejected? There could have been 10 other priorities. There could have been politics at play. What did I learn from that? Next time, I better . . . stack the deck, develop more sponsors around that table.

When I've developed this muscle, inevitably in those darkest of moments, the most politically thick moments, the worst case ends up being "they will fire me." So if they fire me because I did this, I don't want to work for this organization anyway! Why am I worried about not advancing this, not standing up for this person? Not doing this thing, crossing this line that I'm nervous about? So the tip is play it out. What's the best that can happen? What's the worst that can happen? You will find that the worst-case outcome in your mind has slim probability. You may take a political hit. I have trained myself to do this in seconds and minutes. Before, I would write it all out in pros and cons. To frame it in best that can happen versus worst that can happen, it takes you down the path of, and then what . . . and then what . . . and then what? It trains you to isolate the fear, summon your courage, and make clearheaded decisions about the best path forward, while being amply prepared for a myriad of outcomes.

# BECOMING "COMPETENTLY COURAGEOUS"

Jim Detert is the author of *Choosing Courage* and the John L. Colley Professor of Business Administration at the University of Virginia's Darden School of Business. He researches what he calls the "competently courageous"—people who create the right conditions for action by establishing a strong internal reputation and by improving their fallback options in case things go poorly.

The competently courageous carefully choose their battles, discerning whether a given opportunity to act makes sense in light of their values, the timing, and their broader objectives; they maximize the odds of in-the-moment success by managing the messaging and emotions; and they follow up to preserve relationships and marshal commitment. Four principles surfaced from Dr. Detert's research that can help you improve your chances of creating positive change when you do decide to act, employing certain behaviors, according to his book.

## Principle 1: Lay the Groundwork for Taking Action

- Employees whose workplace courage produces good results have often spent months or years establishing that they excel at their jobs, that they are invested in the organization, and that they're evenhanded.
- They've demonstrated that they're able to stand both apart from and with those whose support they need. In doing so, they've accumulated what psychologists call "idiosyncrasy credits"—a stock of goodwill derived from their history of competence and conformity— which they can cash in when challenging norms or those with more power. (We've also seen the reverse: When people with a reputation for selfishness or ill will stand up for legitimately needed change, they tend to be less successful.)

## Principle 2: Choose Your Battles

- Not every opportunity to display courage is worth taking. Ask yourself two questions before moving ahead: Is this really important? Is this the right time?
- As you gauge whether an issue is truly important, be aware of your emotional triggers; allow yourself to be informed but not held hostage by them.
- Observe what is going on around you, and if the timing doesn't look right, hold off. Scan the environment for events and trends that could support your efforts, make the most of an organizational change or the appearance of a new ally, for example.

## Principle 3: Persuade in the Moment

When you are ready to take action, Dr. Detert wants you to focus primarily on:

- Framing your issue in terms that the audience will relate to
- Making effective use of data
- Managing the emotions in the room. Connect your agenda to the organization's priorities or values, or explain how it addresses critical areas of concern for stakeholders. Ensure that decision makers feel included—not attacked or pushed aside.

## Principle 4: Follow Up

Those who exhibit competent courage follow up after they take action, no matter how things turned out. Here's what you want to do after you have spoken up:

- Manage your relationships with the people involved.
- When things go well, thank your supporters and share credit.
- When things go badly, address lingering emotions and repair ties with those who might be hurt or angry.

Follow-up also means continuing to pursue your agenda beyond the first big moment of action. Dr. Detert reminds us that even when their initial steps go well, the competently courageous

> continue to advocate, reach out to secure resources, and make sure others deliver on promises. And when things don't go well, take it in stride, view setbacks as learning opportunities rather than hiding from the fallout or giving up. . . . Above all, keep your values and purpose front and center. You'll have a stronger sense of self-respect through any setbacks you face, and you'll be less likely to regret your actions, no matter how things turn out.

In metamorphosing into your competently courageous self, you will need to return to your best self over and over and check in with the list from your Arrive and Thrive Values Tool™ as you speak up and practice competence in taking courageous action.

# CULTIVATING A CULTURE OF COURAGE

The first time Janet started to think about courage as an important leadership attribute, she was running her first big national practice.

> We had an outside evaluator who evaluates businesses give me feedback of what they were hearing from our clients about us—what they said was, "We love working with Deloitte and we think it is a wonderful firm, but Deloitte's greatest attribute is their greatest weakness; that they are too nice." This idea of telling people what they need to hear, not what they want to hear, was feedback. That was a really important moment. I took that feedback and in helping my colleagues think about how we could be stronger consultants, but also, how we develop people in taking that exact frame of feedback from this evaluator.

Cultivating a culture of courage is an important attribute for an organization. This means you look at how you and others interface with clients and each other and have the courage to gracefully speak your mind in a variety of situations. These situations can include giving feedback to a client or individual developmental feedback, including when you thought a conversation was going astray about a strategic direction. Being thoughtful about how to have courageous conversations is important as you lead and develop others.

With that, let's talk a little about a larger audience or the public eye. Being straightforward in a well-informed manner around the things that are important for others to know is the kindest, gentlest, and most humane thing to do.

Janet has witnessed and been part of situations where it has been easier to kick the can down the road versus having the tough courageous conversations, be it with a partner, a member of her team, or a client. "I have come to see that the ability to be direct, clear, and straightforward in a gracious manner helps the situation advance to a better end-state and creates the best outcomes."

Having courageous conversations in response to social justice movements, business leaders, including Janet, have taken a step back to analyze their organizations' current diversity, equity, and inclusion (DEI) practices. "While I have always encouraged disruptive decision-making on my teams and been a fierce advocate for inclusion, I knew this was a moment where we needed to sit back and listen and learn rather than make any immediate decisions. I am a firm believer that we must listen louder than we speak, and we must train our ears so that when others speak, we really, truly listen."

Addressing how we as leaders have fallen short in combating racial inequities in the past is difficult work. Taking actionable steps toward a more equitable and inclusive future is one way as a business leader Janet has committed to DEI. By tackling these issues head-on, we can show that, despite fears surrounding doing or saying the wrong thing, taking action and listening will allay the "scariness" and build our resilience and commitment.

We are inspired by another story shared by Salesforce President and CFO Amy Weaver that signifies a culture of courage:

> I think the most powerful speech I ever gave in terms of impact to other people was with my whole global team about four years ago. I was expected to give this inspirational speech, and what I talked about instead for five minutes was three major failures in my life. One was, I made a mistake that almost cost an IPO. I had to fix it and get past it. Another, I was involved in a deal in which everything went wrong. I had to get up every morning and sludge through until it got done. Third, I had my hat in the ring for a board of directors' seat for a significant foundation. I was so excited. It was a stretch. There were thousands of people. I got down to number two and didn't get it. I was so crushed. In talking to my teams

about these mistakes, I emphasized that you fix them and get over it. Other people will make mistakes; help them get through. You can do everything right and not get it at the end, and you're going to try again. You could feel the change in the room and the teams after that speech. We created something called the moonshot program. I told people to come up with moonshots, and dedicated funding for quarterly moonshot programs that were game-changing. We knew going in they may not work but we also knew they would make us a better department by finding the courage to innovate.

## AUTHORS' PICKS:
### Our Favorite Tools and Best Advice for Cultivating Courage

### Lynn Loves Issue Selling

Issue selling is a strategy that empowers you to navigate situations that demand courage. It is defined as a process by which individuals influence others' attention and understanding of events, developments, and trends that have implications for leaders and the organization's performance. Issue selling requires courage because when you believe you have something (an idea, a product, a vision) worthy of the attention of another, it will mean you are taking risks and standing up and out for what you believe in. Others may or may not buy in, so courage is needed.

Adapted from the article, "Get the Boss to Buy In: Learn to Sell Your Ideas up the Chain of Command," by Susan Ashford and James Detert in *Harvard Business Review*, issue selling entails:

1. Doing your homework by understanding the context, conducting research, and collecting data so that you can package, tailor, and educate your audience about the issue.

2. Being strategic about framing the issue and telling the story so that it is presented as a win-win, important investment, or urgent need.
3. Managing the power and politics associated with the issue and realizing there are emotions associated with the multiple perspectives/views about the issue.
4. Knowing timing matters by taking into account the rhythm of organizational life, trends, and deadlines.
5. Having a coalition of people who can provide you with an honest opinion about the issue and be early supporters.
6. Understanding the organization's culture for selling issues as it relates to formal and informal approaches.
7. Being solution-centric by not only presenting an issue, but by also having a solution and pathway of action to achieve the solution.

Issue selling succeeds when you:

- Care about and identify with the issue
- Have a positive relationship with the audience
- Feel psychologically safe

## THRIVER'S WISDOM

### No Time for Fear in the Nonprofit World: Natalie Martinez

Centered on empowerment of girls, college-aged women and professional women through intensive mentorship programs, Strong Women Strong Girls (SWSG) personifies courage in making a difference in 1,200-plus lives annually since 2004.

As with any organization, it starts with an exemplary leader. CEO Natalie Martinez directly ties her courageous actions to the young women who will ultimately benefit from the results. In fact, she doesn't allow herself to miss an opportunity to exhibit the fortitude she has spent a lifetime molding. Here, she shares tips on how to take courageous actions.

## The Courage to Do Things Differently

In any position I've ever been in, my approach is never to do things just because that's how it's been done in the past. We should always bring a fresh approach and question everything. No matter the job or who the people are above me, no matter if I'm the only Black person in the room, I've had to say to myself, "This is the right thing to do." I've had to dig deep within my gut, stand on what I believe in, and move forward in that way. I've also had to have the courage to sit in rooms with people who I find are intimidating to me and who are not like me, and advocate for the right thing to do. It's not always something that is provocative like improving diversity in an organization. It can be as simple as saying no to spending budget on something that will not benefit our program marketing. To challenge the status quo, I've had to lean into my skills and abilities that are not stamped by education or approved by a certain title or role but rather that come naturally to who I am.

## Devise and Protect a Strategic Plan

Throughout my career I've learned I have this ability to see organizational structure and know what is needed to make things come together to be successful. For example, I knew at the start of the Covid-19 pandemic that we needed to do a strategic plan because waiting for the pandemic to be over would mean not surviving. Because we had a strategic plan, we were able to message to our funders and community partners what we were doing so it protected us during a tumultuous time.

## Allow Your Personal Experiences to Guide You to a Greater Mission

I represent African Americans. That's the perspective I come from and the knowledge and culture I draw from—but it hasn't always been easy to be a woman of color in any room. Whether it's in a boardroom, at a roundtable discussion with other professionals, or leading a team with diverse backgrounds, I've often found myself in the minority. I've had to find the courage to be my authentic self and to stand up for what I believe in. I have to push program managers when they want to do curriculum a certain kind of way, push college mentors to bring every single thing they are doing back to the girls even though there is a social justice element to our work. I've gone through what these girls are going through and I have that perspective. You don't have to be from the background I came from to possess this ability. Recognizing your circumstances is key to it all. How do you use that thing in your toolbox? I look at the things in my toolbox, the grit that comes from being Natalie, and its pieces in my toolbox. At the end of the day, you must have a winning attitude.

## Keep Fighting Obstacles

Less than 10 percent of fundraised dollars go to nonprofits created for people of color and less than 1 percent goes to nonprofits run by women of color. Black-led organizations have unrestricted net assets that are 76 percent smaller than their white-led counterparts. This gap in support for Black-led organizations is the adversity that matters the most to the success of SWSG. Being a woman of color and having to fundraise in Boston where there is a ton of old money and old boys' networks has been excruciating. I came to my position with fundraising experience, but I didn't have access to the philanthropic network that has been in place in the city for decades. I am a leader of a nonprofit that is in desperate need of operating dollars. The truth is, securing general operating support is all about establishing a trust relationship with the company or foundation and this requires faith in leadership. This, for me, is funders saying "I trust you as the leader to do whatever you need with these dollars." To break through the bias about my identity and earn the faith of donors is a challenge I face on a regular basis as I lead SWSG. I have to keep fighting against these barriers to demonstrate that our organization is trustworthy and viable and able to make an impact for the girls and women we serve. We *do* make impact, and we will continue to!

## POWER RECAP Cultivating Courage

### Key Points About This Practice

- Courage is the ability to do something that frightens you.
- Impact comes out of making difficult decisions.
- Growth, innovation, and transformation result from being courageous.
- If you are not able to enact courage to have a conversation or take action, the effects are significant.
- Big picture, purpose, making a difference in others' lives, and doing the right thing all fuel the courage to take risks.

- Acknowledging when you don't know something sets up conditions for receiving support.

- Growth mindset creates a passion for learning rather than a hunger for approval.

## Suggested Actions

- Acknowledge when you don't know and ask for help.

- Lay the groundwork for others to demonstrate courage.

- If you are facing conflict, ask yourself before acting: Is this really important? Is this the right time?

- Identify your emotional triggers. (What's the story behind how you are feeling?)

- Thank someone for being courageous today.

# FOSTERING RESILIENCE

*Our resilience strengthens with every challenge, every situation we endure. It always ends. Welcome what's next.*

**Whitney Johnson, author, *Disrupt Yourself***

## BOUNCING BACK

Where would we be if we couldn't get back up after being knocked down? Living through the global pandemic has been one long journey of resilience and at every level: individual resilience, family resilience, organizational resilience, community resilience, national resilience, and more. These days especially, there is no shortage of discussion about the criticality of resilience. Yet fostering it? Must we? And how do we?

*Fostering resilience* means proactively preparing for the often unexpected twists and turns that life brings, and rising up through challenges stronger and wiser. Resilience is the ability to bounce back and adapt. It requires agility. With every bounce back, you become a better version of your best self. The greatest gift of this practice is the opportunity to deepen your own inner journey and self-understanding while also leaning *out* and *on* others for support along the way.

If you are a woman leader, chances are you have already built the muscle of resilience. If you are a woman of color or identify as other than straight and Caucasian, you know resilience. If you are managing multiple identities and/or none of them is what you find when you look at the dominant identity in leadership power in your organization or context, then you know resilience. While the pandemic forced the job of adapting well in the face of adversity to be a skill for every leader on the planet, we women needed no health crisis to recognize the import of agility. In many ways, anyone who has faced adversity or strife already knows how to adapt and pivot in the face of hardship. Yet what does it mean to foster resilience in a way that enables you to lead even more powerfully? Why must women especially be intentional about fostering resilience?

Resilience is essential because humans need strength to process and overcome hardship. If you don't foster resilience, you run the risk of:

1. A toll on your physical and mental health
2. A decline of your self-esteem if you are unable to confront barriers that seek to disempower you, such as negative energy or difficult people
3. Not allowing yourself to stretch and grow
4. Locking yourself out of opportunities

Resilience is typically defined as the capacity to recover from difficult life events. Fostering resilience is about embracing reinvention, which does not have to accompany a frequent major overhaul. What may be frequent is the consequential practice of self-empowerment, self-assurance and alignment as change knocks on your door or opens another one beckoning you to walk through.

## Resilience Defined

- Persevering and experiencing a growth trajectory in the middle of challenges, changes, disruptions, and adversity
- Bouncing back after challenges and adversity so that you can not only survive but also thrive
- Having the fortitude to make positive adjustments, adapt, and be agile in the midst of a challenging situation
- Mobilizing your resources, capacity, and strengths to overcome adversity or change

"Resilience is doing well when you shouldn't be doing well. Resilience is your ability to withstand adversity, bounce back from hardships, and grow despite life's downturns," says Amit Sood, MD, the executive director of the Global Center for Resiliency and Wellbeing, and former professor of medicine at the Mayo Clinic in Rochester, Minnesota. Three key insights drive the approach that Dr. Sood created:

- The human brain spends more than 50 percent of its time with a wandering attention processing neutral or negative thoughts; this predisposition fatigues and stresses our brain.
- To recharge, the brain needs rest, uplifting emotions, and motivation every 60 to 90 minutes.
- Creatively designed and thoughtfully implemented practices that help you develop intentional attention and resilient mindset can produce remarkably positive results with minimal time commitment.

According to Dr. Sood, resilience isn't a *fixed trait*. Flexibility, adaptability, and perseverance can help people tap into their resilience by changing certain thoughts and behaviors.

Dr. Sood believes "we are all strong in different ways. Some of us keep a cool head in any argument. Some of us are good at listening. Some of us are good at having a positive outlook when faced with a negative situation. Some of us are good at speaking up and raising our voices when something's not right. Some of us are good at recognizing when to let things go. All of our strengths make us resilient and help us cope with the stress we face." Turning back to Practice 1 on best self, the great news is that the most resilient among us have a lot of strengths.

One leader who embodies a lot of strengths and thrives on exercising resilience is Gail Boudreaux, president and CEO of Anthem. As both an athlete holding numerous records for stellar performance in the basketball arena and a top health care leader, having served as executive for several industry giants, Gail practices the game of resilience based on firsthand experience, no playbooks. She says she does not consider losses "defeats." They are exercises in resilience. Gail asserts:

> Certainly, there is disappointment when something doesn't work out the way you wanted it to, but it allows you to think harder and deeper about the next move. What in my thinking was wrong? The best example came amidst the Covid-19 pandemic, which was more about stopping and listening. I spent more time listening to our associates—and I've always believed in strong communication—but we talked a lot. At one time, we were doing phone calls three times a week. The information sharing was so important. There was so much uncertainty in the world and in our business, and we shared every day as resilient leaders. We were crystallized in the activities, and we got less in the intensity and pace as time went on, but we've used that to communicate where we're heading in our vision and our goals. We've kept listening.
>
> Often as CEOs, we feel we should know the path and have all the answers. For women in particular, it's even more

important because there are not that many female leaders. People expect us to be always the best, but we learn as we come up the ranks. It's a competition. I've seen that your resilience comes from something whether it's from sports or from having other experiences in your life. It shows you that failure is never forever. There is always something else.

## HOW TO RISE WITH GREATER RESILIENCE

In challenging times, you most likely desire to return to a steady state, but what if instead your goal becomes turning the crisis into an opportunity? How do you take what is broken and make something different and beautiful? The truth is, you don't always know when you'll be called to a different stage (in love, life, work, geographically, etc.) or when a different stage has just called you. To foster resilience, the best concepts we can offer to you will mean learning about:

1. Four modes of action required to foster resilience
2. Becoming a positive deviant
3. Creating circles of support
4. Fostering well-being
5. Understanding resilience using the "S Curve"

## FOUR MODES OF ACTION TO FOSTER RESILIENCE

Lynn has found in her crisis leadership research (with Erika James) four modes of action we navigate when faced with a challenge, change, disruption, or adversity. They include noticing fear, pausing for rejuvenation and reflective sense-making, learning, and applying all of this in action to foster ongoing growth.

## Noticing Fear

It is normal and expected to at first meet a challenge with feelings that are generated from fear. It could mean a full amygdala hijack (as we discussed in Practice 1 as the fight-or-flight response that takes place when you are faced with a perceived threat) or mean any of the following might show up:

- Paralysis
- Denial
- Anxiety
- Panic
- Negative energy
- Anger
- Guilt
- Unhappiness
- Judgment
- Shame

And lead you to do fear-based behaviors like:

- Hoarding resources
- Inaction
- Thinking myopically
- Lacking emotional intelligence/being insensitive to your impact on others
- Selfishly focusing on yourself

Most people eventually are motivated to move out of these states, and yet many don't know how. If we are living a life of self-awareness and paying attention to when we are kicked out of our best self (triggered), then we *will* notice fear. The first step is noticing fear, and the next is calling a time out for yourself before you respond to or *act* from that fear. This is where pausing comes in.

## Pausing for Restoration and Reflective Sense-Making

We need to pause for restoration and reflective sense-making. Taking the pause allows us to return to our best self *before* we take action so that when we do, we act with intention and effectiveness. To activate the pause in a way that is restorative to you, it's a great idea to audit your energy. (Stay tuned for Susan's exclusive tool, the Micro Energy Audit.)

## Draw Plans for Your Restoration Inner Work Room

Fostering resilience begins with your inner work. It might not be convenient or even interesting to you, but you'll need to "double down" on the relationship you have with yourself. She's the one who has so much wisdom that often you overlook. Reflective sense-making requires you to begin with you. See and own inquiry as your gateway to continual improvement. You won't be sorry. You'll be remarkably resilient! Ask yourself some reflective questions, such as:

- What's going on?
- What do I need to learn?
- Why is this happening to me? (Or even, why is this happening to the world?)
- What's the pathway moving forward so I can be the comeback kid, and what do I need?
- What systems (or requests) do I need to make for it to work?
- What's triggering this disruption? What's the change or trigger?

Allow yourself downtime to do your work and restore. Give yourself *grace*, or the courtesy of goodwill and understanding. What do I need to learn to be resilient? Listen to the whispers of your heart. You must understand your superpowers to get up when you're down. We addressed how to discover and return to your best self in Practice 1. It is essential to understand the trigger that causes the rut; these triggers might be your best clues to how to more thoughtfully manage yourself in times when resilience is called for.

In taking the pause, you may wish to incorporate a quick, 15-minute meditation, or even just close your eyes and take four deep breaths. Getting grounded in your body *matters* and we know meditation calms the mind.

## Begin a Daily Mindfulness Practice

Neurologists, psychologists, and other mental health practitioners agree on the effectiveness of meditation in reducing physical, mental, and emotional disturbances. In fact, the brains of long-term meditation practitioners look more like the brains of people much younger, according to the BrainAGE Index and corresponding study by Drs. Eileen Luders, Nicolas Cherbuin, and Christian Gaser. Show us a leader who doesn't want to arrive and thrive with a younger but still equally brilliant brain to go with that leadership opportunity! In essence, meditation promotes mental balance by controlling the "monkey mind," essentially a colloquial term for the brain activity known as the "default mode network" (DMN). The DMN is responsible for what we think when we do not attend to anything specific. It causes the mind to wander and engage in nontargeted pieces of information that distract us. Reduced DMN activity in the brain is the reason why meditators can remain more present-oriented and focused. When we dedicate ourselves to daily meditation, we can feel more insightful of the self and surroundings, be more empathetic and self-compassionate, and develop more positive connections with each other. Meditation also leaves its mark on the medial prefrontal cortex, commonly known as the "me center," which is the brain site responsible for our perceptions, understanding, and knowledge, emphasizes research in the "Mind, Mindfulness and the Social Brain" report published by *Indian Journal of Social Psychiatry*.

Most important, and as it relates to fostering resilience, meditation impacts our mental health by regulating the functioning of the ventromedial cortex, dorsomedial cortex, amygdala, and insula, all of which are specialized brain centers that regulate our emotions, reactions to anxiety, fear, and bodily sensations of pain, hunger, and thirst, according to Dr. Thanh-Lan Ngo, medical chief of the Mood Disorder Clinic of Hôpital du Sacré-Coeur de Montréal. Her definition of mindfulness encompasses attention, intention, curiosity, and benevolence, which is the perfect benchmark for your chronicles of resilience.

### Learning
The learning mode is acquiring the knowledge to be resilient and thrive in your new normal. This may take the form of perspective taking, contextualizing your world, scanning for possibilities and scenario planning, crafting a theory of change, acquiring knowledge through learning activities, resources, and partners, and prototyping possibilities.

### Fostering Ongoing Growth
The growth mode is doing the work to be resilient; it is about taking action. These actions will be largely informed by your learning and might take the form of developing collaborative relationships, seeking ways to best be in service to others, and taking on stretch assignments and experiments. An example is being intentional about scheduling time quarterly with a mentor who really energizes you and helps expand your perspective.

## BECOME THE POSITIVE DEVIANT

As you embark on the learning and growth stages of the four modes of action to foster resilience, a terrific way to navigate with a positive outcome in mind is to practice the art of positive deviance.

Positive deviance refers to a behavioral and social change approach that is premised on the observation that in any context, certain individuals confronting similar challenges, constraints, and resource deprivations to their peers will nonetheless employ uncommon but successful behaviors or strategies that enable them to find better solutions. The creator of the positive deviance approach, Jerry Sternin, says "In every group there are a minority of people who find *better* and more successful *solutions* to the challenges at hand . . . even though they have access to *exactly the same resources* as the rest of the group, their uncommon practices or behaviors allow them to flourish."

Through the study of these individuals (subjects referred to as "positive deviants"), the positive deviance approach suggests that innovative solutions to challenges may be identified and refined from their outlying behavior. Your goal is to foster your muscle of resilience such that you can be the positive deviant in any situation you find yourself in. Positive deviance is more than surviving. It is thriving while being resilient.

Perhaps positive psychologist Dr. Jeremy Sutton, sums it up best, with resilience as the centerpiece: "Positive deviance is perhaps better thought of as a positive mindset rather than a model or theory. Its strengths are its simplicity, widespread applicability, and brevity. The approach is ideal for facing an intractable problem requiring a solution that includes social and behavioral change."

In their book *The Power of Positive Deviance: How Unlikely Innovators Solve the World's Toughest Problems*, authors Richard Pascale, Jerry Sternin, and Monique Sternin set forth the four Ds central to delivering a positive deviance outcome: define, determine, discover, and design.

### Step 1. Define the problem and the necessary outcome.

The impacted group (rather than a set of outsiders) defines, refines, and reframes the issue by engaging with one another to understand the data that measures the problem and creates a view of how an improved or ideal future would look, for example.

**Step 2. Determine common practices.** The impacted group is most qualified to determine commonplace practices and behaviors. Set up meetings to include different partnerships inside the group. Equally involve everyone in identifying activities, learnings, and prioritization.

**Step 3. Discover uncommon, successful behaviors.** Identify who in the impacted group faces the same challenges with the same resources, yet tackles the problem successfully. Then share the lessons.

**Step 4. Design an initiative using the learnings.** Begin small, then expand the rollout. Connect people who were not previously connected. Create opportunities for learning to take place. The impacted group itself will monitor the overall effectiveness of the initiative. If successful, document the insights gained and suggested behavior, and share beyond the original community to others facing similar challenges.

## CREATING CIRCLES OF SUPPORT

Babson College professors Drs. Rob Cross and Danna Greenberg, along with former *Harvard Business Review* editor Karen Dillon, assert that "Resilience is not purely an individual characteristic, but it is enabled by strong relationships and networks." In their 2021 article "The Secret to Building Resilience," the authors report early findings of their research that points to how we can become more resilient in the process of connecting with others in our most challenging times.

In working with women over the years at Simmons University, we have found that women specifically need to be very intentional about building a support system. We often do this more thoughtfully or organically in our personal lives but not in our professional lives. Women can and do build support systems through connection with other women, and through contextually supportive nonwork arenas like our communities of faith or children's school communities or our own family communities. We have support in our lives.

You *must* lean on wise elders and wise others. You need connectors, you need mavens, the collectors of information; you need mentors, sponsors and coaches. You need mentees (those wise youngers will teach you a lot!). Candidly, helping women to rely more on others could be an entire book in and of itself. The importance here is how seriously you need to take the intentional cultivation of support from others. As always, we are big proponents of inquiry that easily deepens each of the 7 Practices. As such, ask yourself:

- Who do I need on my personal board of directors?
- From whom can I source best practices?
- Who are those people who have gone through what I'm going through? Who can give me perspective?
- Who do I need to know geographically or locally?
- What resources do I need? How can I get help?
- How do I need to adapt to receive the help I need?

## FOSTERING WELL-BEING

Remember that in Chapter 1, Dr. Richard Safeer gave us all a sigh of relief in stating that we do not have to navigate laborious lists of "best self" items created by others; that we must define our own self-journey? Resilience is cojoined with best self, emphasizes Dr. Safeer. He adds: "While it is helpful to have dedicated time to attend to your own needs, you don't necessarily need to carve out time for well-being. You do need to identify opportunities to *practice* well-being. It isn't necessarily having to go to the gym. Well-being needs to be part of your day, all day, and thriving is an advanced state of well-being."

Someone could feel well yet feel they haven't achieved their full state of potential. At a higher state of well-being, you aren't judging yourself over your state of well-being; you spend more time comfortable and happy than not. Dr. Safeer reminds us that judgement is not an attribute that is consistent with a higher state of well-being.

## Our Well-Being Is Always in Flux

Our well-being is highly dependent on the people around us and the cultures where we live. By cultures, Dr. Safeer is referring to the common behaviors and beliefs of those with whom we share commonalities. We are part of many sub-cultures ranging from community, our work/organizational cultures, our family cultures and even the culture of our closest relationships. The common sets of values and beliefs that keep us together or drive us apart underpin our well-being.

## The Role of Self-Care

Self-care is the act of getting to a better place of well-being. How you define self-care might be going to a spa weekend with your friends or having a weekly family dinner. It might be keeping up with annual health check-ups or giving yourself time to talk on the phone with an old friend once a week. Your self-care might be moving your body X times a week or eating foods that you enjoy. The bottom line: Dr. Safeer suggests that your self-care is up to you and should be based on your well-being needs.

## When Dealing with Adversity, Expect Your Affect to Be . . . OFF

When a leader shows up and is not in a positive state of well-being, however that leader defines what that means for herself, it will impact everyone. A state of ease, however, seems like a tall order with the very natural and real stressors of life, relationships, and leadership. Dr. Safeer suggests leaders need to go back to the basics of self-care in order to quell the very real stressors that come with high-level executive roles. Of course, there is a litany of lists of strategies and techniques such as learning to say "no," getting enough sleep, exercising, etc. Assuming you are practicing all of the best elements of self-care, Dr. Safeer urges you to pay attention to a few higher-level cognitive themes, that while hardly ground shaking, are often overlooked or underutilized:

- Prioritizing
- Delegating and then trusting (letting go)
- Setting boundaries
- Staying in the present (being mindful)
- Putting life in perspective

Deloitte Chief Well-being Officer and coauthor of *Work Better Together* Jen Fisher agrees with Dr. Safeer's themes and cautions you to refrain from negotiating your time away and wants you to say yes to what really matters.

Jen believes that practicing wellness so you have the resilience life requires—at its simplest—is a daily commitment to eat (well), sleep (7 to 9 hours), move (in whatever way you enjoy), and find joy (in the moment). She says, "Especially as women, we have been led to believe that taking care of ourselves is somehow selfish and it is something we do only when we are tired and exhausted and having feelings of burnout." Jen believes a big component and perhaps the most important aspect of well-being and resilience is cultivating strong relationships. Jen and her coauthor Anh Phillips assert that authentic, trust-based relationships increase job satisfaction, engagement, productivity, and retention—and even decrease healthcare costs. Jen's work underscores the importance of creating circles of support. She says:

Well-being is what allows you to be resilient. When you're taking care of yourself and you're in a good place physically, emotionally, mentally, and spiritually, you are much more able to adapt and be agile to whatever the challenges are in your life. You can think more clearly and react more clearly. You are far more easily equipped to pull out of the forces of disruption. Well-being is a daily pursuit.

## UNDERSTANDING RESILIENCE USING THE S CURVE

We haven't yet used the term "disruption" to describe the signature reason for resilience. That's because it belongs here with Whitney Johnson. Whitney is both a self-disruptor and among the world's leading thinkers on disruption. She helps high-growth organizations manage change by developing high-growth, change resilient individuals. She is the award-winning author of several bestsellers, a world-class keynote speaker, frequent lecturer for Harvard Business School's Corporate Learning, and an executive coach and advisor to CEOs. As a former Wall Street stock analyst, Whitney understands momentum and growth. She was an Institutional Investor–ranked equity research analyst for eight consecutive years and was rated a superior stock picker by StarMine. Whitney knows resilience!

Whitney also has an important perspective on thriving:

When people say, "I will survive," or "I'm a survivor," they may be stuck in survivor mode. That can work, but it doesn't lead to a life of happiness. I don't think that is where we do our best work. We require resilience to disrupt us from mere survival to a place where we can thrive, so we are living and working in *that* place. We have moments where we're forced to focus on survival, but ideally that's not our general

mentality. The S Curve of Learning can help us visualize the
process that will move us from stuck to unstuck, developing
resilience along the way.

Sociologist E. M. Rogers popularized the S Curve in 1962 as
a graphic illustration of how disruptive new ideas and products
spread through cultures. Whitney's insight is that the S Curve can
be applied to individuals too, as a model for the process of learning and growth. Progress on a new learning curve is relatively slow
at the base of the S until, as competence and confidence increase, a
tipping point is reached. On the steep back of the curve, growth is
rapid and rewarding. But then growth slows again, as the potential
for progress on a particular S Curve is exhausted. We can become
bored, stagnant, and disengaged. The plateau becomes a dangerous precipice.

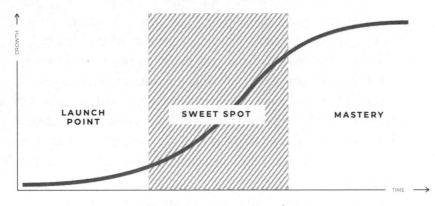

**FIGURE 4.1** Original S-Curve

Whitney explains:

When we understand how something works, we can proactively affect it. Understanding how growth works increases our capacity to optimize self-directed growth, and to help others in their development. For example, knowing that progress is slow and often painful at the beginning of something new can help us be resilient and persevere through the difficulty. Resilience isn't something we are born with. It's fostered as circumstances require it. To succeed at something new, we gradually gain resilience through the difficulty. When others are struggling, we can encourage rather than criticize, because we expect opposition to be part of the learning process.

In the sweet spot of the S Curve of Learning progress is much faster. We've accumulated resources in the form of knowledge, expertise, and support. Our efforts are more rapidly rewarded.

The sweet spot is a fun place to be in the growth process. We do our best work there. We thrive. The goal is to extend this productive phase of the curve for as long as we can. We don't feel the need for resilience as much as we did before, but it's important here too. We need to volunteer for challenging opportunities and get involved in stretch projects. The greatest growth occurs when facing opposition. When the opposition of the launch point has dissipated, we need to be strong enough to impose some on ourselves. We want to keep the curve challenging. In essence, we need to make it harder than it has become and stick with it.

"Eventually, though, we're going to reach the mastery phase and growth will slow again," Whitney says. "We've learned most of what we can on a particular S Curve. It's easy to coast, but counterproductive to the process of growth. This is where personal disruption to start again at the launch point of a new S Curve of Learning is necessary. But it isn't always, or even often, easy. Think like a surfer; when we get to the top of a wave, we're soon going to have to start at the bottom of another wave. Resilience is required to proactively embrace change by leaving a place of familiarity and comfort to launch into the unfamiliar and uncomfortable again."

Whitney reminds us that a setback (she prefers step back) can be exactly what we need to thrive again. "Sometimes we're forced to do something new—sooner or later all of us are. We don't always get to choose. A firing, a layoff, failed business, contrary personal circumstances—any of these or others can disrupt us. This both requires and strengthens resilience. A new S Curve of Learning is an opportunity to build new competence and confidence, even when we undertake it against our own will. Using the S Curve of Learning model can help us build resilience by giving us a clear way to think about both the ups and downs of making progress. And progress is a fundamental human yearning."

## WHITNEY'S 10 TIPS FOR RIDING THE S CURVE FOR MAXIMUM RESILIENCE

1. No matter where you are on your S Curve of Learning, or what challenges you face, you can thrive by focusing on growth rather than survival.
2. Watch for signs of momentum. Especially in the launch point, where it's hard to see progress, look for little signs that some growth is being achieved.
3. In the sweet spot, find ways to keep challenging yourself. Stay in learning mode; don't shift to performance mode or perfection mode.

4. As you increase in competence, you may be asked to do more than you can. Stay focused on your main objective. Learn to say no when it's the right answer to a demand on your time.

5. Mistakes and even failures are good teachers. Learn to learn from them. Recognize that falling short is an important step in building a long-term track record of success.

6. Have important conversations early and often with partners, bosses, and others who are invested in your growth, or in whose growth you are invested.

7. Blame and shame are enemies of resilience. Don't indulge in them yourself or visit them on others.

8. Receive feedback graciously and act on it as appropriate.

9. Continue to pursue your own growth, even when confronted with injustice.

10. Develop resilience, not excuses, to help you face opposition.

## AUTHORS' PICKS:
### Our Favorite Tools and Best Advice for Fostering Resilience

### Susan Loves the Micro Energy Audit

The Micro Energy Audit is taking pause to look at how you are in the moment. What emotions might you be experiencing? Are you tense, worried? How does your body feel? Are you present in the moment with who is there and what you're discussing, or are you distracted? Just notice.

When you find yourself navigating a life challenge or disruption, you can expect your energy to be off. This is normal. The name of the game is to get going intentionally and productively again. This Micro Energy Audit is a pause and a self-check to be sure you're taking yourself into consideration as you live out your day. You need not wait for a challenge to check in with yourself. On an ideal moment on an ideal day, you are speaking, behaving, making choices from a place of intention. You are aware of your thoughts and feelings and how they might inform your actions. You consciously return to a place of being intentional. That's the goal, and this goal requires inner work.

## Lynn Loves the Resiliency Diagnostic

Confidence in your abilities is like taking a multivitamin with breakfast to start your day. It's a boost, it's a burst. Confidence gives us the capacity to be resilient. Confidence narrows the gap between the paralyzing effect that change can cause and the action to ensure, adapt, bounce back. It's not easy to monitor our level of confidence if we are not examining the skill or perspective that coincides with a situation. Enter the Resiliency Diagnostic.

The Resiliency Diagnostic, which I codesigned with organizational psychologist and Dean of the Wharton School of the University of Pennsylvania Erika James, was created to assess your confidence to recover quickly from a crisis, disruption, or change. The diagnostic has 20 questions with six themes about how you are holding up and learning in high-pressure situations, and the behaviors needed not only to survive but also to thrive:

1. **Embracing change:** crises are change events we often are not prepared for. People who can get past the initial reaction of fear and discomfort to see opportunities are able to embrace change.
2. **Checking your alignment:** aligning your values, strengths, and identity as resources for resiliency.
3. **Monitoring physical, mental and emotional well-being:** so you have the energy to manage challenges.

Check your level of confidence with the skill or perspective listed.
Take note of confidence gaps and focus on further developing those skills.

| EFFECTIVE CRISIS LEADERSHIP COMPETENCY | I need to develop this skill | I'm moderately comfortable with this skill but could develop more | I am confident I have this skill in my toolbox |
|---|---|---|---|
| 1   I see change as opportunity. It does not make me anxious. | | | |
| 2   I know how to assess a situation and understand what is happening. | | | |
| 3   I am clear about my values and what matters to me regardless of what is changing around me. | | | |
| 4   I regularly assess my strengths and developmental needs. | | | |
| 5   I see change as a chance to learn new skills, experiment and build my expertise and value. | | | |
| 6   I direct my own career trajectory and choices. I am consciously scanning for opportunities to develop. | | | |
| 7   I have healthy physical, mental, and emotional habits that I can maintain during a crisis. | | | |
| 8   I have tools at my disposal for managing emotional dysregulation – intense negative emotions during stressful situations. | | | |
| 9   I make time for learning and reflection. | | | |
| 10  I have strong empathy skills. | | | |
| 11  I have relationships that sustain me during times of crisis. | | | |
| 12  I am comfortable with my personal identity and can differentiate who I am from the work that I choose to do. | | | |
| 13  I have networks and affiliations that keep me connected to the world and informed about things that are important to me. | | | |
| 14  My professional relationships are broad and varied. | | | |
| 15  I am clear about how my skills could be transferable to other roles or situations. I know my skillset will give me flexibility and I can adapt to change. | | | |
| 16  I have a safety net and feel that I can weather a crisis. | | | |
| 17  I have designed my life knowing that I may have to adapt to change. | | | |
| 18  I know how to determine what is in my control and what is not in my control. | | | |
| 19  I regularly seek out new challenges that stretch beyond my comfort zone. | | | |
| 20  I regularly ask other people for feedback to help me learn, grow, and adapt. | | | |

**FIGURE 4.2**  Resiliency Diagnostic

© 2010–2020 Erika Hayes James, PhD and Lynn Perry Wooten, PhD

4. **Committing to continuous learning and reflection:** by updating your knowledge, skill set, and perspectives, you will be better prepared for resiliency.
5. **Broadening your networks and sources of information:** so you have the support of people and access to knowledge needed for resilient actions.
6. **Planning for adapting:** plan for the changing circumstances by stockpiling resources and redesigning your work and personal life.

Based upon the responses to the questions, you can identify confidence gaps for resiliency and craft action plans for closing the confidence gaps.

## Janet Loves the Resiliency Road Map

Janet embraces the Deloitte point of view on building a resiliency road map: how leaders can not only bounce back but bounce up from adversity. As a core human trait, resilience is written into our DNA, a default code that helps us survive and adapt in the face of disruptions large and small. Given its central role in human flourishing, resilience has been studied across the fields of positive, cognitive, and clinical psychology. For decades, researchers have also studied it through the prism of neuroscience, coaching, leadership, and philosophy. This key attribute has been put to the test, as 2020 and the Covid-19 crisis made resilience scholars out of just about everyone.

Yet resilience is more than meets the eye. Certainly, it's about bouncing back from disruptions and adversities. Indeed, this *bounce-back* notion is a commonly understood definition of resilience. But resilience also serves a higher function and value. Ultimately, it's about bouncing out of self-limiting thinking and paradigms, and bouncing up to our highest levels of potential and our most magnetic, impactful realization of leadership. This is the path of self-transcendence.

Deloitte's resilience perspective spans the three human dimensions—or realms—where resilience happens (or not) in real life. With this model as a guide, leaders can learn and practice the makings and moves of whole-person resilience.

**The personal realm** is the domain of self-awareness and self-mastery. It pertains to exercising sagelike self-command and aligning your life and work with your deepest, most authentic values.

**The interpersonal realm** is all about relationship mastery. Specifically, do your relationships provide a deep, fulfilling sense of connection? A crucial component is the relationship-formative role of communication, including the importance of the ways you show up for people's good news, as well as difficult conversations.

**The extrapersonal realm** comprises the external environmental conditions that need to be navigated across nature, society, and work to bolster resilience and achieve broader impact and legacy. In addition to navigating external conditions, executives and leaders have expansive influence over forming these conditions for others.

Just as adversities in real life often overlap, the three realms also act interdependently. Explore how these dimensions arise in relationships. For example, in the interpersonal realm, focus on the ability to build and nurture supportive, authentic relationships based in empathy, shared values, and constructive communication. In the extrapersonal realm, think about environmental agility—the ability to sense the health of environmental conditions and mitigate the impact of suboptimal life and workplace forces.

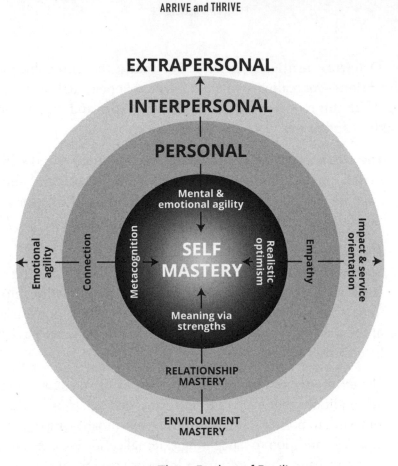

**FIGURE 4.3** Three Realms of Resilience

© 2021 Deloitte Development LLC

When whole-person resilience is in place (see Figure 4.3), it opens the door for optimized behaviors and results. It also allows leaders to activate a resilience strategy, more effectively guide others, boost productivity, and build high-performing teams. What's more, by incorporating these methods into daily practices, leaders can also challenge belief systems that might be holding themselves and their organizations back.

To create resilience habits, leaders have to keep practicing and actively trigger their brains to remain aware of the continuous changes within and around them.

## THRIVER'S WISDOM

### Thriving in Six Industries: Beth Ford

President and CEO of Land O'Lakes Inc. Beth Ford was an early starter and riser in resilience as the fifth of eight children growing up in Sioux City, Iowa. She says she had no choice but to be resilient! Being competitive with siblings, even if simply elbowing others out for the last piece of chicken at dinner, taught Beth that when the going gets tough, you've got to stand up for yourself, dust yourself off when you encounter a stumbling block, and keep moving ahead. Here, she offers her tips for rising resiliently.

### Strength, Determination, and Grit Go Far

One of my greatest role models and inspirations as it relates to the importance and magic of resilience is my mother. She raised us while getting her registered nursing license, then went on to get her master's degree, switched directions completely and became a psychologist and a therapist, and finally decided to become a minister to round out her career. She literally worked with people on their mind, body, and soul, and worked harder than anyone I know. That was a firsthand, in-depth case study in strength, determination, and grit that influenced not only how I looked at the world, but how I showed up in it. As a result, I've now worked in seven positions spanning six different industries and can say I've gotten to where I am today in large part thanks to those lessons. Navigating both upward and lateral moves in a number of industries reiterated the importance of resilience, a sense of humor, and the motivation to keep trying.

## Turn Setbacks into Opportunities

A lot of times in business (and definitely in my own career journey), we are disappointed by a job or opportunity we wanted but didn't get. Oftentimes that's through no fault of our own, but rather because a manager or leader didn't feel we were right for the position at that moment in time. What I had to learn from those experiences was that it usually didn't have anything to do with my own strengths or skills, but because I just wasn't the right person for that particular job. Let me tell you: that's a hard message to hear and accept, and an even harder one to shake off. You can't take those decisions personally. Like my mom always said, "You didn't get stupid overnight." It's not for lack of skill, work ethic, or motivation, but perhaps due to timing and circumstance.

I decided to take these "setbacks" and use them as opportunities. I asked questions and worked to understand why I wasn't the candidate they were currently looking for, and also sought to understand what it would take to become the candidate they were searching for someday.

## Resilience Boosts Confidence

Resilience is the trait that builds confidence. Resilience is the trait that helps you cast aside self-doubt and try again. It's the trait that teaches you how to be creative, innovative, agile, and persistent. It forces you to question yourself and your situations, and constantly strive to improve.

Often, and definitely much more in the past, women remained more passive and silent when it came to what they wanted. Now, women are speaking up for what they want out of their career and out of their life. I was always taught to ask for what I wanted because no one was going to read my mind. This is absolutely critical, and resilience is what keeps us confident, gives us the courage to ask for what we want and deserve, and keeps us moving forward.

**Resilience Can Be Modeled**

Be true to yourself. Bringing your full, authentic self to life and work, along with being resilient, is critical. Also, work your plan with confidence and encourage others to do the same. Success isn't a zero-sum game. Instilling confidence and encouraging resilience among your friends, family, and team members will only lead to greater success for everyone.

## POWER RECAP Fostering Resilience

### Key Points About This Practice

- Resilience is the ability to bounce back (and up) and adapt.
- Humans need strength to process and overcome hardship.
- Change brings practice in self-empowerment, self-assurance, and alignment.
- Resilience requires flexibility and adaptability.
- If you practice self-awareness, you can more easily notice fear, pause for reflective sense-making, and act.
- Allow yourself downtime for restoration.
- Meditation positively impacts your mental health.
- Strong networks and relationships help you build resilience.

## Suggested Actions

- Establish your daily mindfulness practice.

- Form a new collaborative relationship, whether to be in service of others or to take on a new stretch assignment.

- Identify your community of mentors, sponsors, mavens, and connectors.

- Share your lessons.

- Consult the S Curve to determine where you are and how best to prepare with resilience for where you are heading.

# INSPIRING A BOLD VISION

*The essence of leadership is your ability to engage others in a compelling vision. This is what a leader does.*

—Albert Bourla, Chairman and CEO, Pfizer

## THE PRACTICE OF
## USHERING IN CHANGE

*Inspiring a bold vision* is a discovery of what needs to change (it could be seeing a way to innovate, solve a problem, or fundamentally reconstruct something for the better), and then finding the courage to embark on the essential steps to bring the change to life. It begins with *noticing*. Have you thought about having your business enter a new market not pursued previously, but should for future growth? Has someone pointed out to you a feature to a product that clients don't use, and if retired, would save money? Have you ever wanted to flip a process on its head because you know it would improve efficiencies and team dynamics? Your noticing might be because you discover a needed change and figure out how best to change it, or because others have pointed out a problem and offered a solution (or an altogether new venture).

Sometimes, the vision is to improve upon something that is seemingly "unbroken" to those around you. It can be viewed as highly disruptive, but you (or someone on your team) strongly believes it's essential for the health of the business in the longer term. No matter, this awareness becomes a choice of focus and a direction—and then you stand up for it and lead the way to the better outcome. *Doing that is acting boldly.*

Inspiring a vision, however, doesn't mean you must become a visionary. To be bold is to have the courage to flex the muscles you have honed working the first four practices. Boldly doing anything is about taking risks with confidence. Like the other practices, inspiring a bold vision will only work if you lean in and on others. In fact, providing stretch assignments for team members and putting them in nonobvious roles can be a great instigator to vision as well to get everyone's creative juices flowing.

In the words of Simmons University President Emerita Helen Drinan, "Boldly inspiring vision is a skill that can be developed. I learned it by doing it, first in small efforts, for example, at the department level, and then over time, in large strategic efforts at the organizational level. It's not that you are a born visionary; rather, you gain in courage and confidence through the experience of increasingly successful vision launches."

When the coauthors of the international bestselling book *The Leadership Challenge* Jim Kouzes and Barry Posner first set out to discover what effective leaders do when they're at their personal best, they collected thousands of stories from ordinary people— the moments they recalled when asked to think of a peak leadership experience. Despite differences in culture, gender, age, and other variables, these "personal best" stories revealed similar patterns of behavior. They went on to call these the Five Practices of Exemplary Leadership®, and one of the five is, *inspire a shared vision.*

On the companion website to their book, Kouzes and Posner describe the practice of inspiring a shared vision as, "Leaders passionately believe they can make a difference. They envision the future and create an ideal and unique image of what the organization can become. Through their magnetism and persuasion, leaders enlist others in their dreams. They breathe life into their visions and get people to see exciting possibilities for the future."

The fascinating news about the data Kouzes and Posner have gleaned from their multirater assessment on the Five Practices of Exemplary Leadership® is that inspiring a shared vision is the lowest-scored practice for women *and* men. This raises the often discussed "cloud" that seems to surround the topic of women and vision. To cut to the chase here, more evidence than not suggests women are as capable as men in boldly inspiring vision. There are, however, some interesting nuances.

Since the publication of the notable article "Women and the Vision Thing" in *Harvard Business Review* revealed that women scored lower on "envisioning"—defined by the authors as "the ability to recognize new opportunities and trends in the environment and develop a new strategic direction for an enterprise"—the narrative about women being shy to express a bold vision has continued. Data from this research suggested that women might be more collaborative in the way they do visioning, which tends to diminish the extent to which people see women as visionary. What this means for you is that you will want to use the word *vision* very deliberately and claim visioning as one of your skills.

Albert Bourla, CEO of Pfizer, who consistently inspires colleagues around a vision for changing patients' lives by driving the scientific and commercial innovation needed to have a transformational impact on human health, laments the fact that even today women are often asked to do more to prove themselves than men are. This societal double standard is in direct contrast to Pfizer's commitment to equity, which is one of the four values that Albert established for the company shortly after becoming CEO.

We need to shed old ways of thinking—conscious or unconscious—that prevent us from being truly equitable. This includes confronting the cynicism born of an establishment traditionally led by men. When we do this, we create an environment where bold leaders—regardless of gender—can inspire their teams to aim high and to accomplish more than they ever imagined they were capable of.

Women's leadership expert and founder of The Cru and bestselling author of *Drop the Ball* Tiffany Dufu wants you to remember that women are socially conditioned to be collaborative, generous, nice, and liked. What this means is that you are not necessarily rewarded in all contexts to be competitive in the ways men are.

She clarifies, "To have vision is to say, 'I have an idea of what the world needs that trumps what everyone else on the planet is doing and, in some ways, the best idea to move us forward.' Women shy away from this declaration if it is deemed too self-aggrandizing. The bottom line is that it's difficult for women to be bold about a vision."

But difficulty does not correlate to stagnancy or not enacting vision in our powerful sphere of arriving and thriving. In fact, Tiffany emphasizes that the noticing, making observations, is your entry ticket. She advises:

> You need to be a student of society, humanity. You need to be someone who desires to make observations of human beings. There isn't a product or service that isn't rooted to human behavior. If you listen to someone talking about their story, you will learn what informs them, their mindset. Especially for those who are successful. How do they make decisions? How do they behave? When I connect with another woman, I am interested in her challenges. What

does she think is blocking her? What is the story that she is telling about herself?

People who are able to articulate vision are people who are students and are very curious about humans, behavior, what makes us tick. If you read enough books, have conversations with people, then you can develop patterns and notice a need to fill and a new way to fill it. They call you a visionary, but really, it's as if you've had hundreds of conversations. It's curiosity and hunger to learn more from a network that informs you that causes you to make observations and ultimately new pathways.

A network for building a vision is not incidental. The offering of this practice boils down to believing in yourself and trusting your judgment as you enroll others, organize a path that will reach the desired destination, and be the one who harnesses the energy of others to achieve it.

Vision is especially urgent during a crisis—the most recent being caused by the global pandemic, which we will likely still be navigating for years to come. Lynn states: "The call for leadership has never been more acutely felt. In all corners of life and society, leaders are wanted not just to reassure but to paint a picture of what is next. How will we overcome?"

## BOLDLY BOLSTER THIS PRACTICE

Inspiring a bold vision suggests implicitly that you need not be the visionary or the one with the brilliant ideas. In case this has you concerned, we believe you don't have to always be the one who has the vision, but you *do* need to be able to enroll others in it and create inspiration around it. As Anthem's Gail Boudreaux shared with us, "When you spend the time building a vision, it's about communicating it and listening and making sure people get it. And saying it again and refining it and working with others to make it even bolder." Janet adds, "Even though I am the person who is accountable to the vision, having the confirmation that others have the sparks, ideas, or get excited about it, generates the forward momentum needed." So cultivating this will entail:

- Having a team with diversity of experiences, skills, and thought
- Deeply listening to others around you
- Integrating what you hear and processing what others are saying in a way that adds to your own ideas
- Formulating the narrative of the vision
- Managing the doubters with empathy
- Communicating the vision with bold confidence

If you *are* the person who wakes up with farfetched, seemingly out of reach brilliant ideas, you will want to socialize it, let others weigh in, be open to input, *and* trust your knowing at the same time.

Let's look more deeply at what a vision is, explore your personal leadership vision, then uncover how best to inspire a bold vision at the organizational level.

## What Is a Vision?

Whether you are thinking about creating a vision for yourself or for a team or organization, having a vision is the ability to think about or plan the future with imagination. A vision looks forward and creates a mental image of the ideal state that (an individual, team, unit, or organization) wishes to achieve. It is inspirational and aspirational and grounded in clearly defined values and purpose, which are rapidly escalating in importance.

Simon Sinek, inspirational speaker and author of five books, including *Start with Why* and *The Infinite Game*, says, "People don't buy *what* you do, they buy *why* you do it." Following this statement, a few contemporary companies that have been recognized for how they articulate their vision are Nike (if you have a body, you are an athlete), Patagonia (designing and manufacturing best garments while also inspiring solutions for the environment), PayPal (democratize financial services), TED (spread ideas), and Honest Tea (catering to taste, catering to health).

No matter the size and scope of the vision, it should be centered on projecting goals and future potential within the context of your current business environment. Showing that clear alignment can help you bring people along on the journey. This sometimes manifests as a courageous conversation (refer to Practice 3 for more insight).

By nature, vision is energizing and demonstrates real results of real efforts—it's not a dream or hope. The constructive change that you are building toward focuses on small details that accumulate and quicken the heart in excitement upon manifestation. The process of building is cumulative and keeps you going.

## INSPIRING A BOLD VISION FOR YOURSELF

You're not starting from scratch; you're starting from experience. Sally Helgesen, cited in *Forbes* as the world's premier expert on women's leadership, is an international bestselling author, speaker, and leadership coach. She says, "Building a vision often begins with a personal vision. People's capacity to care is personal. Formulating a destination for yourself begins with asking yourself some tough questions—and giving yourself the time and space to foster clarity."

Sally wants you to look deeply at yourself to learn the art of inspiring a bold vision. What exactly is it that you're seeking to contribute to the world? You must do this internal work and home in on what it is that you wish to achieve or contribute. Then ask yourself, how would this serve the world? The risk you run if you don't ask yourself these questions begins and ends with regret. You spin your wheels, you tell yourself when you see success elsewhere that you "could have done that, too." Sally suggests having a statement of intention, an aspiration. Oh, and vague responses are unacceptable! What is the one thing you are trying to contribute? What's your larger purpose on the planet and in your lifetime? Building a bold vision and inspiring others about it ideally starts from your recognition about what you want for yourself.

As spotlighted in *Harvard Business Review*, Wharton organizational psychologist Dr. Steward Friedman, who researches and writes about leadership and work/life integration, suggests that to build your personal vision, you must be able to describe a compelling image of an achievable future.

> Leadership vision is an essential means for focusing attention on what matters most; what you want to accomplish in your life and what kind of leader you wish to be. A useful vision has to be rooted in your past, address the future, and deal with today's realities. It represents who you are and what you stand for. It inspires you, and the people whose commitment you need, to act to make constructive change towards a future you all want to see.

Dr. Friedman suggests four key components to a personal leadership vision:

- A compelling story of the future is engaging; it captures the heart, forces you to pay attention. Those who hear it want to be a part of it somehow. And they are moved.
- What does your future look like? What's the billboard image? If others could travel into the future with you, what would they find? A well-crafted leadership vision is described in concrete terms that are easy to visualize and remember.
- The story of your future should be a stretch, but it must be achievable, too. If it were not achievable, you would have little motivation to even bother trying.

- Finally, future simply means "out there," some time from this moment forward, but not so far away that it's out of reach.

In her book *Mastering Your Inner Critic*, Susan addresses the hurdle of *clarity* and wants you to clarify what you're up for. The big opportunity is to purposefully keep an eye on achieving what you really want for yourself. How can you create a promising future in which you are intentional about your professional advancement? She offers several tools and practices, including more from her friends Tara Swart and purpose guru Richard Leider, pinpointing how you can manifest what you really want. Susan's core advice is:

1. Listen to the whispers of your heart, focus on where your unique gifts and talents are in service of others and discover the power of purpose.
2. Create ways to ensure your work allows for this part of you to show up at least some of the time.
3. Make time for reflection and discussion.

With the clarity of a curated vision for yourself in hand, let's turn now to inspiring a bold vision as an organizational leader.

## INSPIRING A BOLD VISION FOR THE ORGANIZATION

"To inspire a bold vision, you must be comfortable with your ambition and have conviction," says Tiffany Dufu. This is key, as ambivalence does not go into any formula for success.

If we distill all of our experiences, the conversations that we have had with executives in preparing this book, and all of the best research on inspiring vision available, you will find that inspiring a bold vision for the organization boils down to these four principles (or subpractices):

- Being clear about your organization's purpose and "why"
- Listening with humility for brilliant ideas, recognizing the value of new insight and, if it sticks, deliberately exploring possibilities
- Having courage to take a leap of faith, freely walking into the unknown
- Communicating with enthusiasm about what you know, what you don't know, and the path forward

Inspiring a bold vision for the organization is the ability to articulate the path forward crisply and confidently, including what you know and what you don't know. You need to be able to communicate what the path forward means for the business and, at the level of organizational leadership, what the path forward means for your business communities. With this, having the humility to listen to a wide set of voices and knowing that you must move forward with imperfect information will be essential.

Even the most confident leaders are dealing with incredibly imperfect information. The ability to listen to a wide variety of sources, synthesize, and have enough confidence—but also have humility to help set a path without knowing all the answers and every level of detail and how things are going to turn out—is the other skill that matters most when boldly articulating vision.

Lynn's story of leading a vision in less than perfect times is when she began the Simmons presidency in the middle of the pandemic, a social reckoning, and economic uncertainty.

> The university was operating remotely, and higher education was being disrupted with a shift in modalities for delivering education to students. Although I was leading in a challenging time, I knew that a vision was essential because a vision inspires bold thoughts and actions, provides a road map

for seeing possibilities, and invites stakeholders to share in achieving goals. To create the vision, it was an inward and outward process that entailed sense-making of our ecosystem and understanding the needs of our community. At the core of the vision was resiliency, well-being, and everyday leadership. Bringing this vision to life entailed inclusive practices and teamwork as we reimagined our operations and positioned the university for our new world. As a result, we spent much of our time learning, experimenting, and embracing change.

The Deloitte *2021 Global Marketing Trends: Find Your Focus* study found that organizations that know why they exist and who they're built to serve may be uniquely positioned to navigate unprecedented change. The global pandemic was the biggest reset for brands in a century. Almost overnight, companies have had to change how they create content, market services, distribute products, and take care of newly remote teams. Yet purpose-driven companies are likely already better positioned to ride out this time of extraordinary change—they know why they exist and who they're built to serve, regardless of what they sell today.

Referring to one of the core Business Chemistry work styles as defined by Deloitte (see Practice 1), if you are a Driver and you can execute, vision might be a scary concept. Don't let it be. As you take broader responsibilities, you must cultivate the ability to communicate where you want the team to go and why. That is what vision is. It answers: What is the direction of travel? What do you want the team to do to get from here to there? That is not a far cry from being really good at driving and executing because a lot of driving and executing is refining and clarifying.

## Grounding Your Vision in Purpose

Connecting to broader organizational purpose illustrates how your vision contributes to improving broader societal issues and is connected to the long-term value your organization brings. It can create a sense of belonging and empowerment of "leaving it better than we found it." Janet coined a leadership principle for her teams which is "we are they." It stems from an experience leading a new area of business where the overwhelming mindset was one of defensiveness and a lot of "*they* said I couldn't" and "I tried but *they* didn't listen." Janet's immediate reaction was there is no "they." "We are they." It was a message of empowerment to raise flags and be inspired to devise solutions. We are all responsible. We are all accountable. We all must lead. So we all must approach every issue in our workplaces as an issue deserving of our attention.

Connecting to broader purpose is also so important in the retention of talent. Case in point: Deloitte's *2021 Global Millennial Survey* revealed that younger generations (Gen Z and Millennials) want to work for companies with a purpose beyond profit—companies that share their values—and that they feel more empowered to make a difference as part of organizations. It's critical, but an area that still needs focus—as fewer than half of Gen Z and millennials surveyed see business as a force for good in society, and 7 in 10 millennials feel that businesses focus on their own agendas rather than considering the wider society.

Simon Sinek might recommend when it comes to inspiring a bold vision you should think about your organizational *why*. To elaborate on this point introduced earlier when describing what vision is, Sinek maintains that people don't buy *what* you do, they buy *why* you do it. "Very few people or companies can clearly articulate *why* they do *what* they do. By *why* I mean your purpose, cause, or belief; *why* does your company exist? *Why* do you get out of bed every morning? And *why* should anyone care?" The profound insight that Sinek offers can help you as you listen and communicate vision. When it comes to organizational values or guiding principles, Sinek maintains that to be truly effective they must be verbs. This also provides a great clue as you look to inspire a bold vision. By switching to verbs, he means "It's not *integrity*, it's *always do the right thing*. It's not *innovation*, it's *look at the problem from a different angle*. Articulating your organizational values as verbs gives your stakeholders a clear idea of how to act in any situation."

Importantly, remember to direct your courage to the intention and action of taking a leap of faith. And we agree with Albert Bourla in that the correct dosage of courage may need to be commensurate with just how bold the vision is.

He says, "The bolder the vision, the more the concept of inspiration has to be there; you need to be someone who can take others and drive them there. You need to convince them, uplift them to go there. That's a very important thing." Can you relate to Albert's thinking here? Have you had a leader who inspired you to think bigger? Albert tells us:

> I truly believe that people don't actually know what they can and cannot do. As a leader myself, this is a constant theme. Usually, you severely underestimate what can be done. When you're setting goals or visions, you tend to set something that is believable, that the others can come with you to achieve—let's underpromise and overdeliver. When you underpromise, usually you deliver less than if you had overpromised and you stretch yourself. This is the piece people are missing. If you want to thrive and excel, you should overpromise. The delivery will always be more. In the end, what counts is the outcomes. It's not what you promised. Every leader should have an audacious, ambitious goal and try to get people there.

It's also important to consider how much optimism versus pessimism you bring to a situation as a leader. Janet says:

> There is a part of me that thinks through what may go wrong, but that is counterbalanced by enthusiasm about

new things and where we might be able to take them. For me, that balance has worked well. Even the people who wake up with brilliant ideas have no idea how to get it done. I am about setting really clear and exciting ambitions, but then very quickly turning that into what are the five things we need to get started or what might the ten steps look like along the way.

Part of inspiring people with a vision is not only painting it but helping them understand how they participate in it, and how you get from here to there with optimism and enthusiasm.

Communicating with enthusiasm about what you know, what you don't know, and the path forward, requires honing the art of clarifying and communicating. A compelling story of the future is engaging; it captures the heart, forces you to pay attention. Those who hear it want to be a part of it somehow. And they are moved. What does your future look like? What's the image? If others could travel into the future with you, what would they find? A well-crafted leadership vision is described in concrete terms that are easy to visualize and remember.

## INTRIGUE AND INSPIRATION: JANET'S PERSONAL ACCOUNT

A strong example of leading vision is the start of an organization within our business called Deloitte Digital, which has quite a strong brand in the market now. I had taken over running our technology business and some of my team was talking about using digital devices in ways that were fundamentally different than how I had thought about Deloitte's services in a business environment. My Wall Street "back-office brain" didn't compute how these devices would enable business to operate in a fundamentally different way, but I was intrigued.

I was asked and agreed to meet with a potential acquisition target, who within a couple of hours helped me see what was possible. I got the threads to know there was something special and began to build a team that could help me paint the picture of what it could be and what mattered. It went from nothing to a multi-billion-dollar business in five years.

That acquisition target that became the start to Deloitte Digital was sold to us because (1) they felt I understood their vision for the business (I listened) and (2) they felt my enthusiasm for what was possible.

This is an example of creating a vision not because I had the content, but because I listened and trusted the wisdom of the people on my team. I may not be the person who wakes up in the middle of the night with the brilliant idea, but I am able to write and talk about something very compelling by generating enthusiasm, listening, connecting dots, being comfortable without knowing what the full end is going to be (because I certainly didn't, in this example, have any idea what the full end could be). I knew this was something interesting and we could get people excited about it.

## AUTHORS' PICK:
## Our Favorite Tools and Best Advice for Inspiring a Bold Vision

### Lynn and Susan Love the Leadership Practices Inventory

If you're looking for specificity as to what you might be seen doing if you hone the practice of inspiring a bold vision, look no further than at Kouzes and Posner's work. Following their massive research effort that led to the Five Practices of Exemplary Leadership®, they created the Leadership Practices Inventory® (LPI), a multirater assessment tool that asks questions assessing

30 behaviors, containing a subscale for each of the five practices. The six behavioral indicators that suggest a leader is able to inspire a shared vision include:

- I talk about future trends that will influence how our work gets done.
- I describe a compelling image of what our future could be.
- I appeal to others to share an exciting future dream.
- I show others how their long-term interests can be realized by enlisting in a common vision.
- I paint the "big picture" of what we aspire to accomplish.
- I speak with genuine conviction about the higher meaning and purpose of our work.

In uncertain times, you can still intentionally work at honing your skill and practice each of these six vision-sharing behaviors.

## THRIVER'S WISDOM

### Doing Well by Doing Good: Helen Drinan

President of Simmons University for 12 years, Helen Drinan inspired several bold visions over the course of her career as a thriver. Prior to higher education, she worked at BankBoston Corporation for 20 years. She is a firm believer in fixating on a vision and taking risks that may be unpopular until the vision comes to fruition. Here is her advice on all things vision.

### Ground Your Vision in Data

At BankBoston, I worked for a CEO who set an aspirational vision for the corporation to succeed for our shareholders by being the best in the industry at exceeding customer expectations. As the leader for Human Resources, I was responsible for responding to the CEO's call to set in motion a vision that would inspire the workforce to play its role in the corporate vision: what kind of environment motivates the people of an organization to be so committed that they deliver for customers all the time at the highest possible levels? Long before employee engagement was a well utilized strategy in American business, this was indeed a very bold—even transformative—vision. But to ensure the vision deserved the large investment in the integrated set of plans that were required to support it, solid grounding in financial viability was required, and we met that requirement through measurable analytics which demonstrated that capable, committed employees did indeed drive higher levels of customer delight and share of financial business.

## Start with Culture

To be clear to a large organization that you are launching a transformative vision, you need to signal over and over that a big change is afoot. I proposed that we replace the annual executive golf outing with a service day for the same executive group. Instead of walking out the office as a group with all their golf gear, the top executives walked out in yard work clothes for a day rehabbing an underprivileged children's camp. The message inside the corporation was extraordinary—employees now thought that perhaps, by giving up the exclusivity of golf, leadership was serious about everyone working hard together for common goals. And the message outside the corporation was just as surprising—newspaper front page above-the-fold coverage and photograph of the senior officers on the grounds of the camp doing hard, physical work for a great cause—doing well by doing good. After that day, just about every executive followed suit with service days that cascaded throughout the organization for years to come! Cultures do not change overnight, but signals like this go a long way.

One of the other culture changing things we did was to offer stock options to the entire workforce. Encouraging all members of the workforce to think like owners because they are owners played out quite visibly, with people increasingly focused on business results and stock price activity. Our organization was the only banking institution at the time to include all employees in stock ownership.

## Be out Front with Diversity and Inclusion

BankBoston was an acknowledged leader in diversity long before it became the high visibility challenge we understand it to be today. Putting a stake in the ground for diversity was a statement about doing the right thing both ethically and for the business: doing well by doing good. We were especially out front in the LBGTQ community, at a time when we were pretty much alone. We wanted our workforce to mirror our customers. And in short time, we gained great respect as a community partner, far from the stuffy, exclusive, Boston-Brahmin club we had been reputed to be.

## Be Ready for the Responsibility

When I first became president of Simmons University in 2008, I found myself faced with information that foretold a grim future for the institution. As a tuition dependent, modestly endowed, highly indebted, undifferentiated small private college, revenues were simply not growing quickly enough to cover expenses, and no initiatives were in place to address this ongoing situation. While these circumstances were not unique to Simmons, and reflect the crisis in much of higher education which persists today, they were uniquely my responsibility as president of Simmons, and I took them on with intensity. In the short term, this meant going totally against the culture to solve emergencies, like an inability to meet payroll or a budget that was unachievable. Simultaneously, though, conceptualizing a long term sustainable plan for Simmons that was culturally aware had to be a priority in order to make continuing progress.

We went through a strategic planning effort that had sufficient teeth to deliver real market relevant results while incorporating the kind of process, participation, and decision-making necessary to meet the expectations of an academic audience. Out of it came a vision for the future of the university that contemplated opportunities for differentiation: a nationally distinctive institution offering undergraduate and graduate degrees in fields which improve the human condition while emphasizing educating students for empowerment and leadership.

This vision required specific tactics for execution. Turning around the undergraduate program required a large investment in curriculum redesign and the creation of modern living and learning facilities. The graduate programs, on the other hand, were predominantly in the realm of improving the human condition—fields in high demand, such as nursing, social work, nutrition, library science and applied behavior analysis—and offered great financial potential if larger student markets could be identified well beyond the limited populations in neighboring New England states. The solution to the overarching strategic challenge Simmons faced began to emerge: 1) radically elevate the undergraduate program with a new curriculum and new physical plant investments, seeking to stabilize the size and increase the academic competitiveness of the undergraduate student population with an innovative academic offering as well as a wholly new living and learning environment; and 2) expand delivery of the graduate programs nationwide through online classes for as many graduate programs as were market competitive, generating crucial new funds to subsidize the undergraduate program and afford competitive graduate program investments.

I knew that this new strategy depended almost exclusively on the technology of online, very new to mainstream higher education and as yet unaccepted as an alternative to the traditional academic experience. Committing to this solution required my absolutely nonnegotiable dedication, even if I stood alone in the process.

## Hold Tight to Your Vision for the Long Term

Adopting online education happened in two phases: we first launched our own effort. Internal support for online internally was nonexistent except for the small group of faculty and staff involved with the master's degree we were putting online. Everything worked well other than the marketing: we had a great program, and great students, but only 36 of them. You cannot even cover costs at that level, so we had to shut down.

We refused to let a start-up failure stop us, and had a great piece of luck—a visit from a new company seeking to take graduate education online, 2U, Inc. They offered to take our nurse practitioner program online. With continued community opposition, from faculty to staff to alumni, we had the unreserved support of our nursing faculty. They saw this not only as an opportunity to expand the delivery of the nursing program of which they were so proud, but also as a way to contribute to the nursing shortage in the United States.

Helped significantly by the nursing faculty's endorsement, we expanded to other highly reputed graduate programs, and the success was indisputable. Between 2013 and 2018, Simmons shifted from traditional graduate program delivery only to adding online delivery in every state in the union plus Israel. Revenues in online during this period grew from $4 million to $80 million, nearly matching traditional revenues. In that time, the institutional culture started a gradual shift from absolute opposition to online to willingness to study and understand, preparing Simmons to provide first-class virtual education not only for graduate students, but for undergraduates as well when the pandemic befell the country.

In addition, during these years, the new funds were applied as planned to redesign the undergraduate curriculum in a leadership framework, to acquire playing fields to strengthen our undergraduate athletics programs, and to begin construction on the facilities changes necessary to provide the living and learning environment prospective undergraduate students so need to see in order to commit four years of their lives to Simmons. These combined efforts put Simmons on track for long term sustainability, a prospect the university could never have foreseen in 2008 and an obligation that is hopefully embraced by every future leadership team.

# POWER RECAP Inspiring a Bold Vision

## Key Points About This Practice

- Inspiring a bold vision begins with noticing what needs to change. It does not mean you must become a visionary or have all the answers.

- Inspiring vision requires you to be a continuous student, learning from various outlets.

- To carry a vision forth, you must believe in yourself.

- During times of crisis, vision can lift people up and help them think about what's next, what's possible.

- Enrolling others in a vision requires you to establish trust.

## Suggested Actions

- Ensure you have a team (or begin creating one) with diversity of experiences, skills, and thought.

- Deeply listen to others around you.

- Integrate what you hear and process what others are saying in a way that adds to your own ideas.

- Formulate the narrative of the vision.

- Manage the doubters with empathy.

- Communicate the vision with bold confidence.

# CREATING A HEALTHY TEAM ENVIRONMENT

*The most important thing about creating a healthy team environment is to ensure people feel it is safe to take risks.*
—Linda Henry, CEO, *Boston Globe*

## FORMATION OF A POSITIVE COMPANY CULTURE

The need for connection has never been greater. As a leader, you are facing the very real impact of rising rates of burnout, languishing, and depression at work. Further, fears in our pandemic era range from worries about job security to worries about being left out. These realities make *creating a healthy team environment* that much more pressing.

We can now say for sure that collaboration and high employee engagement positively impact profit, and there are hard costs to organizations should employees be disengaged. In fact, Gallup found that highly engaged teams show 21 percent greater profitability, and teams who score in the top 20 percent in engagement realize a 41 percent reduction in absenteeism and 59 percent less turnover. On the flip side, an exhaustive report by the Engagement Institute (a joint study by the Conference Board, Sirota-Mercer, Deloitte, ROI, The Culture Works and Consulting LLP) found disengaged employees cost US companies up to $550 billion a year.

The offering of this practice is to help you know how best to create a healthy team environment. Leading from the best parts of you (your visionary, resilient, courageous, authentic, and best self), it's time to turn that energy fully on others. Your gutsy, resolute goal: ignite others to lead from their best self with one another. Only when you, the leader, understand that you're not alone but in it with your team and others, and bring your unique best self, including strengths you bring to the table, is your best leadership of a healthy working-together environment sustainable. Team leaders, to be effective, need to know what their people are like, what their people are doing today, how they are feeling, and how they can help as team leader.

## DEVELOPING AND ENCOURAGING THE PRACTICE

As we navigated the best thinking from our own experiences and the experiences of those we interviewed, and looked at the relevant research on healthy teams, what emerged as where we think you can focus to foster a healthy team environment in the most intentional way are our *six essential actions to creating a healthy team environment*. We will dive further into each of these six concepts and provide insights on each. They are:

1. Understand and unleash team member strengths
2. Set team direction and strategy

3. Communicate honestly and convene frequently for service excellence
4. Learn and develop together
5. Make it appreciative
6. Ensure psychological safety

## UNDERSTAND AND UNLEASH TEAM MEMBER STRENGTHS

Gallup emphasizes that "strengths-based teams communicate using a common language grounded in what's good." Gallup is dedicated to bridging the science of analytics with the art of advice and learning and wants us to forget all the greater-than-the-sum-of-its-parts motivational sayings and focus instead on *why* it is imperative to know and support everyone's contributions to the team. Gallup finds that the most engaged and productive teams have three things in common:

- They share a common mission and purpose.
- Collectively, they understand and appreciate each team member's strengths.
- They intentionally use the strengths of each team member.

Gallup's premise is that every individual brings something unique and powerful to the team, and conversely, every individual retains areas where they're just not strong. Further, it is up to you (the leader) to work with the individual to help them know how they naturally excel, where they need help from their teammates, and what shared goals or purpose they're all using a strengths-based approach to achieve. Specifically, we suggest you use a strengths-based approach to *intentionally* promote effective delegation, successful partnerships, and deeper collaboration, among other outcomes.

Based on research as cited in Gallup's *StrengthsFinder 2.0* book with Tom Rath, leaders who regularly focus on individual team member's strengths can make a dramatic difference. When focused on strengths, there is a 1 percent chance that a team member will be disengaged, as opposed to focusing on weaknesses (22 percent). See Figure 6.1 regarding the four domains of leadership strengths as depicted in the StrengthsFinder's work.

| Executing | Influencing | Relationship Building | Strategic Thinking |
|---|---|---|---|
| ACHIEVER® | ACTIVATOR® | ADAPTABILITY® | ANALYTICAL® |
| ARRANGER® | COMMAND® | DEVELOPER® | CONTEXT® |
| BELIEF® | COMMUNICATION® | CONNECTEDNESS® | FUTURISTIC® |
| CONSISTENCY® | COMPETITION® | EMPATHY® | IDEATION® |
| DELIBERATIVE® | MAXIMIZER® | HARMONY® | INPUT® |
| DISCIPLINE® | SELF-ASSURANCE® | INCLUDER® | INTELLECTION® |
| FOCUS® | SIGNIFICANCE® | INDIVIDUALIZATION® | LEARNER® |
| RESPONSIBILITY® | WOO® | POSITIVITY® | STRATEGIC® |
| RESTORATIVE® | | RELATOR® | |

**FIGURE 6.1** The Four Domains of Leadership Strength

Gallup®, CliftonStrengths®, and the CliftonStrengths 34 Themes of Talent are trademarks of Gallup, Inc. All rights reserved.

In Practice 1: Investing in Your Best Self, we went into more detail about how to uncover your strengths as you aim to be in flow. We encourage you to do the same for the members of your team. This includes helping each team member to know the strengths of the other members. As team leader, it is your responsibility to match the right people to the right roles, such that their own strengths can be maximized not just for the benefit of the team and organization but also for team member engagement.

General Chuck Wald, a retired director and leader in Deloitte's government and public services practice, is no stranger to matching roles and responsibilities. He has been charged with these "matches" in his various positions spanning a decorated career in military operations worldwide and then in his capacity as a business executive.

In doing so, General Wald has fine-tuned his own vision for what drives a healthy team:

A healthy team knows: What are the goals? What is the objective? What are we trying to do? What are the expectations? What is the tolerance for failure? And even if we fail, our leader has our back. If you can't communicate that, you won't be effective. Sincerity and empathy are interwoven. There are times when you can't tell "everything" as a leader, but the others can't think that you are holding things back from them because you're insincere. Also, change is tough, and change management is another part of leadership. How do you motivate people to accept change in their best interest? The healthy team leader accounts for all of this.

General Wald's points resonate with us. Without a solid understanding of how to motivate the individuals on your team, it's almost impossible to expect them to thrive during times of organizational change.

## SET TEAM DIRECTION AND STRATEGY

To effectively engage and clarify team direction and strategy, we highly recommend beginning and ending with a spirit of collaboration. In the end, members of the team will need to buy into all of this to effectively stay motivated and engaged.

As we defined in Practice 5: Inspiring a Bold Vision, having a vision is the ability to think about or plan the future with imagination. This can be applied at the individual, team, business unit, or organizational level. We invite you to apply some of the same tools as you engage and clarify your team's purpose and vision. As a refresh, your guiding principles will be:

- Being clear about your organization's purpose and "why"
- Listening with humility for brilliant ideas
- Having courage to take a leap of faith
- Communicating with enthusiasm about what you know, what you don't know, and the path forward

## Establishing a Compelling Direction

A healthy team needs a compelling direction, which states definitively: "This is what we'll achieve, and this is how we'll achieve it." Direction is the reason a team exists—its vision, mission, goals, or aspiration. It provides a purpose for the team members to rally around, and shapes both the team's strategy and tactics.

In thinking through the strategy for a compelling direction, it should be both long- and short-term. Long-term direction might be captured in a formal purpose, vision statement, or aspiration: something for team members to rally around. Short-term direction may be captured by goals or frameworks such as key performance indicators (KPIs) or objectives and key results (OKRs) that describe how the team will make intermediate progress to reach their long-term overarching direction.

A clear direction provides team members with an anchor for their commitment to the team. Consequently, the direction should be framed in ways that encourage team member buy-in. It has long been accepted that an effective direction must be clear and challenging but achievable. Recent thinking also highlights the importance of the direction being meaningful and ethically aligned, as the workforce is becoming increasingly purpose driven. To align with the team's direction, team members must not only understand the mission, but be willing to support it—something that may be largely dependent on the compatibility of their own desires and preferences.

Traditionally, it's the team's leader who provides, inspires, or drives a team's direction; however, a team might also be self-directed, with distributed leadership increasingly recognized as an enabler of team effectiveness. A clear and compelling direction also helps a team understand how it should relate to other teams within the organization, where collaboration might be fruitful, and where the team should work (and negotiate) with others. Teams need the flexibility to respond to the local conditions and their relationship to other teams. It may be advisable for teams to set their own goals and success criteria within overarching strategic parameters established by management. The importance of a compelling direction is further heightened for cross-functional teams, which are likely to be faced with company politics and an environment of competing priorities. Without a strong direction, ideally at a strategic company level, a cross-functional team is unlikely to drive through silos to achieve their objective.

As Deloitte's intensive work on team building and infrastructure has shown, a team with a compelling direction will not only motivate its members but may also inspire support from beyond the team.

## COMMUNICATE HONESTLY AND CONVENE FREQUENTLY FOR SERVICE EXCELLENCE

A survey conducted by Atlassian, a software company that develops collaboration tools, revealed that 1,000 team members across a range of industries found that when honest feedback, mutual respect, and personal openness were encouraged, team members were 80 percent more likely to report higher emotional well-being. If team members aren't feeling good about how they communicate with one another, how can you expect them to perform and service your customer and clients with excellence? What it takes to get the most from your team is the ability to convene often and communicate honestly (even, and especially, when opinions differ).

*The Five Dysfunctions of a Team* by bestselling author Patrick Lencioni outlines the root causes of politics and dysfunction on the teams where you work and the keys to overcoming them. Counter to conventional wisdom, the causes of dysfunction are both identifiable and curable. However, they don't die easily. Making a team functional and cohesive requires levels of courage and discipline that many groups cannot seem to muster. The dysfunctions Lencioni lays out include absence of trust, fear of conflict, lack of commitment, avoidance of accountability, and inattention to results.

- The fear of being vulnerable prevents team members from building trust with each other.
- The desire to preserve artificial harmony stifles productive ideological conflict within the team.
- The lack of clarity or buy-in prevents team members from making decisions they stick to.
- The need to avoid interpersonal discomfort prevents team members from holding each other accountable for their behaviors and performance.
- The pursuit of individual goals and personal status erodes the team's focus on collective success.

The dysfunctions are interpersonal—trusting and managing conflict well—but also require the right intent of team members—focusing on ensuring clarity of mission and focusing on collective results over individual results. All of this requires excellent skills in building trust and in communicating effectively. When there is too little trust in the workplace or with a team, it is a toxic work environment. This is the opposite of our aim for team health.

Dan Helfrich, CEO of Deloitte Consulting LLP, is a big advocate of creating a healthy team environment through the alignment of trust and vulnerability, which he says, "comes in all shapes and sizes—acknowledging mistakes past or present, acknowledging unease and that you are grappling with a decision." For example:

> I often talk with teams, small or big groups, saying, here is what I am wrestling with. "Here is what I'm wrestling with" is a really good way to both demonstrate vulnerability and invite feedback. In my mind, the healthiest team environment invites dialogue and disagreement, acknowledges that some decisions are hard to make and don't have clear black-and-white answers. What that also does over time is culturally builds a healthier team environment that can also transcend individual moments that might not work for an individual or group of individuals on the team.

We so agree with Dan's view. Especially as it relates to inviting dialogue and disagreement—it's so important that all team members feel empowered—even encouraged—to voice constructive critiques. It's what oftentimes leads to the best decisions.

## Assume Positive Intent

Lynn has a value at the university: assume positive intent. Janet has a similar leadership principle well-known to her teams: assume and expect positive intent. Susan has written and spoken publicly about the costs of blaming and shaming (in any relationship). We all agree that coming from a place of assuming positive intent, in which we don't leap to blaming or shaming others but instead lead with curiosity about intention, is a key component of healthy team leadership. If you have ever been disappointed by the actions of another, you know that assuming positive intent is easier said than done. As you look to communicate honestly, fostering a no-blame and no-shame environment is essential and at the heart of our advice about how to begin to foster team-based trust. This means you don't give yourself permission to blame and shame any team member—and you hold others accountable if you see it happening (mistakes are learning opportunities—disappointments are best for private coaching or feedback with individuals).

While to err is human and we can be harsh and unforgiving about our own mistakes, we judge other people's mistakes even more harshly than we judge our own. This double standard is very well documented in scientific research and is called the fundamental attribution error. This phenomenon will absolutely derail efforts to create a healthy team environment. Here's how this plays out: When we make mistakes, we often blame the circumstances of the situation rather than take responsibility for the mistake. When other people make mistakes, we tend to overemphasize the other person's role in that mistake and quickly blame them. As a result, we tend to make assumptions about what led to mistakes made by others ("they had negative intentions," "they clearly don't get it," "it was their fault").

Once these conclusions form in our own minds, we tend to act as if they are true. This double standard can be countered through one simple cognitive shift. Assume positive intent and give others the benefit of the doubt. Assume that they had positive intentions, identify the situational details, and get the bigger picture. When leaders blame and shame, trust erodes.

To put this in further context, Janet shares,

> To assume and expect positive intent from those around you can be the North Star for the big things: decisions around how to shift the business, discussions around social justice and social purpose, conversations around what went wrong and what to do about it. But it goes for the everyday stuff, too: giving and receiving feedback, establishing boundaries, and respecting others' boundaries. When you believe we're in this together, for the long haul and for the right reasons, it makes you a more trusting teammate and more patient leader. It fosters a more productive working environment.

And in the end, it can lead to better outcomes for your team, your organization, and you.

The team will follow the leader's actions. If you struggle yourself with assuming positive intent, we invite you to circle back to Practice 1 where we outlined how to return to your best self. *You can't be operating from your best self **and** be blaming and shaming another at the same time.* Practice this return yourself and ask it from your team members. Model the way. Talk about how you are "assuming positive intent" in a situation or with a comment and show what this looks like (typically, this stance is followed up with a genuine question or set of questions, not interrogation).

We have found that if you lead from a place of (1) giving people the benefit of the doubt and (2) modeling a true learner mindset, you will set the stage for an open, even generous climate of team communication. Healthy conflict is not available unless we assume that every situation is more complicated than one person can see (implicit positive intent) and then respond not with our own advocacy or blame, but with inquiry. As you convene frequently (virtually or in person), open and honest dialogue is essential. When the leader communicates with a specific style, others follow suit.

## LEARN AND DEVELOP TOGETHER

What about learning and developing together fosters a healthy team environment? After all, we have work to do and everyone is already stretched thin, especially with the stressors of our new hybrid working realities.

Investing in your staff's professional development is not only vital for team retention, but we observe a stronger appetite for upskilling than ever before. Assessing the current skills and abilities within a team will enable managers to strategically plan targeted development programs that consider any potential skills gaps. Regular development initiatives can help keep employees motivated, while frequent training programs will also establish regular reevaluation of employees, skills, and processes.

There are two focus areas where we believe you want to aim your team learning and development time and energy. The first is on the team itself. This includes providing education and learning on many of the skills we address in this chapter. The aim with focusing learning and development on the team itself is so that the team works together more effectively so all members can achieve what you set out to accomplish with high engagement and outstanding results. The second focus we believe you want to aim your team learning and development efforts around is on the functional and technical upskilling required to compete and win. By this, we mean having guest speakers, reading assignments, training, and other learning initiatives aimed at everything from competitive innovations to better ways of getting work done.

In the age of disruption, where the only constant is change, continuous learning is essential. Creating an organizational culture of continuous learning is critical in attracting and retaining top talent in an increasingly tight labor market. Beyond the case for talent acquisition, continuous learning is what will help equip entire organizations to change at scale. Setting a vision that celebrates education, innovation, and problem-solving skills in our increasingly complex digital world will differentiate great leaders from good ones and will position business more competitively for the future.

Another aspect to creating healthy teams through continuous learning is to pay attention to job evolution. How often are jobs changing, which ones, and to what degree? Fifty-three percent of respondents to Deloitte's *2020 Global Human Capital Trends* report say that between half and all of their workforce will need to change their skills and capabilities in the next three years. As jobs change, does your investment in organization-wide continuous learning support that evolution? Just tracking the cumulative number of learning hours doesn't address how the organization is being reinvented and adapting to external change. For example, if you aren't seeing productivity gains as a result of new technologies being integrated into the workplace, then you may need to look at how jobs need to shift to take better advantage of those technologies.

# MAKE IT APPRECIATIVE

Positivity strategist Robyn Stratton-Berkessel states:

> An appreciative voice provides safety for others to speak their truths. It is invitational and watchful. An appreciative voice is unhurried and patient. It can reframe situations to be helpful and resourceful. It is flexible. The appreciative voice is inclusive. It acknowledges diversity and identifies opportunities to offer possibilities to hold the space for transformational shifts to emerge.

We have seen the power of appreciation and how it can accelerate the creation of a healthy team. The theory is this: what you focus on, grows. When you train your eye to appreciate, you see there is so much to be appreciated. Think of this to leverage the strengths of your team as a whole and the individual members in it. Stratton-Berkessel adds:

> This is a big shift from the traditional view of organizational life where we're rewarded to focus first on mistakes and problems, while the strengths and best assets get taken for granted. This human pattern is built into our evolutionary need for survival: people shut down (or attack) when faced with threat, and they open up (and include) when they feel safe. When one's mind and heart is open, positive emotions, thoughts, and actions follow.

Stratton-Berkessel's book *Appreciative Inquiry* targets organization development and what the authors call a "strengths revolution," which is a befitting term for what we want to convey in the arrive and thrive arena, too. As she says in her book:

> At its heart, *appreciative inquiry* is about the search for the best in people, their organizations, and the strengths-filled, opportunity-rich world around them. Appreciative inquiry is not so much a shift in the methods and models of organizational change, but appreciative inquiry is a fundamental shift in the overall perspective taken throughout the entire change process to "see" the wholeness of the human system and to "inquire" into that system's strengths, possibilities, and successes.

In a 2017–2018 Deloitte study *The Practical Magic of "Thank You,"* more than 16,000 professionals were surveyed about how they want to be recognized, for what, and by whom. For the day-to-day, the best recognition may be the easiest—say "thank you"! Even when the accomplishment is significant, cash isn't king. Across organizational levels, generations, genders, and Business Chemistry types (revisit Janet's favorite tool for investing in your best self from Practice 1), the most valued kind of recognition is a new growth opportunity. Pioneers, Drivers, and Millennials value these new opportunities even more than others do.

*The Practical Magic of "Thank You"* research also found that big wins aren't the only thing people want to be recognized for. It's also important to recognize the effort they put in (especially Guardians, Integrators, staff, and millennials), their knowledge and expertise (especially Drivers, Guardians, and staff), and their commitment to living the organization's core values (especially Integrators). It matters who's recognizing who, and whether the preference is for recognition from one's direct supervisor, from leadership, or from colleagues depends on who is being recognized, with Business Chemistry types and generations showing particularly meaningful differences. Your appreciation of someone need not be shared with the whole world to make it count. Most people prefer recognition that is either shared with just a few people or delivered privately. Fewer want recognition that is widely shared, Guardians, Integrators, and Baby Boomers, in particular. Bottom line: recognizing people's unique contributions, and doing so in the ways they prefer, is one approach to demonstrating they belong, and to helping them find meaning in their work.

# ENSURE PSYCHOLOGICAL SAFETY

We're living in a world with assorted work environments and formats, thanks to technology, multinational companies, entrepreneurship, and global health crises. No matter what arrangement we're navigating, what do we all want and need first and foremost? Hint: it's not money, and it has many implications.

"Sorting out future work arrangements, and attending to employees' inevitable anxieties about those arrangements, will require managers to rethink and expand one of the strongest proven predictors of team effectiveness: psychological safety," write Amy C. Edmondson and Mark Mortensen for *Harvard Business Review*.

Much of the work done in many organizations is done collaboratively by teams. The team is the molecular unit where real production happens, where innovative ideas are conceived and tested, and where employees experience most of their work. But it's also where interpersonal issues, ill-suited skill sets, and unclear group goals can hinder productivity and cause friction.

## Psychological Safety at Work: Google's Project Aristotle

Following the success of Google's Project Oxygen research where the People Analytics team studied what makes a great manager,

Google researchers applied a similar method to discover the secrets of effective teams at Google. Code-named Project Aristotle, a tribute to Aristotle's quote, "The whole is greater than the sum of its parts" (as the Google researchers believed employees can do more working together than alone), the goal was to answer the question: "What makes a team effective at Google?" The researchers found that what mattered most was how the team worked together, and the most important variable of working together effectively was the presence of psychological safety.

Organizational behavioral scientist Amy Edmondson of Harvard first introduced the construct of "team psychological safety" and defined it as "a shared belief held by members of a team that the team is safe for interpersonal risk taking." In a team with high psychological safety, teammates feel safe to take risks around their team members. They feel confident that no one on the team will embarrass or punish anyone else for admitting a mistake, asking a question, or offering a new idea.

To illustrate what psychological safety means in action, here is the list of questions Edmondson asked to measure a team's level of psychological safety. Team members were asked how strongly they agreed or disagreed with these statements:

1. If you make a mistake on this team, it is often held against you.
2. Members of this team can bring up problems and tough issues.
3. People on this team sometimes reject others for being different.
4. It is safe to take a risk on this team.
5. It is difficult to ask other members of this team for help.
6. No one on this team would deliberately act in a way that undermines my efforts.
7. Working with members of this team, my unique skills and talents are valued and utilized.

The preceding list of questions might be helpful in your pursuit in having meaningful conversations with team members, but we will cut to the chase. In her TEDx talk, Edmondson offers three simple things individuals can do to foster team psychological safety:

1. Frame the work as a learning problem, not an execution problem.
2. Acknowledge your own fallibility.
3. Model curiosity and ask lots of questions.

Of the six essential actions to creating a healthy team environment presented in this chapter, we posit that the final essential action of ensuring psychological safety is the only one that, if absent, kills the effectiveness of the team even if the other five are present.

A tip for greatly increasing your ability to ensure psychological safety is to reflect on your own state of being at any given time while working. How intertwined is your personal life and leadership impact? *Wellbeing at Work* author and chief scientist workplace for Gallup Jim Harter says *very*.

> Our careers impact all the other areas of our lives. We don't come to work as robots, we come to work as human beings. If we have bad relationships at work, we're going to take that home with us. Numerous studies show that our work environments affect our physiology and risk of disease. They affect how we view ourselves, the opportunities for involvement in our community, and how we partner with people with similar passions as us.

# AUTHORS' PICK:
## Our Favorite Tools and Best Advice for Creating a Healthy Team Environment

### We Love: Team Strengths Exercise

Executive advisor and performance coach Bill Flynn, author of *Further, Faster: The Vital Few Steps That Take the Guesswork out of Growth*, created a team exercise that we love, based on *The Five Dysfunctions of a Team* by bestselling author Patrick Lencioni. Here is what Bill wants us to do to go further, faster in developing our team's strengths when in a team retreat or quarterly meeting. Before facilitating the team strengths exercise, Bill suggests conducting an icebreaker asking some personal questions to evoke some empathy for and from members of your team. Ask each member to share the following:

- Where were you born?
- How many kids are in your family?
- Please describe something you had to overcome in your childhood.

Team strengths facilitated exercise directions:

1. Ask each team member to devote one Post-it note to each person on the team by writing their name at the top.
2. On the Post-it, write three things that person does that makes the team better.
3. On the same Post-it note, write one thing that person could do to make the team *even better* (for this, focus on a strength that may be underutilized).
4. Last, write down on a final Post-it note one thing *you* could do to make the team even better.

Each member of the team takes a turn to hear what every other member has to say about them. Their job while others share the three strengths and one "even better if" is to listen and to capture the feedback from their team members and end by sharing a commitment about the one thing they will focus on to do *even better*. At subsequent meetings, each person provides an update on the commitment they made, and the team provides supportive feedback.

## We Love: The Core Purpose Exercise

When it comes to the purpose of your team or the team "why," we turn again to Simon Sinek, who has a core purpose exercise that we modified slightly to help you engage your team in your team *why*. We recommend that you assign this to team members to do individually and then bring them together to debrief and discuss. We have found it is ideal to have an "outside" facilitator (or a non-team member or expert facilitator) to manage the discussion to a positive outcome.

**Step 1:** Write down what your team does.

**Step 2:** Ask why that is important.

**Step 3:** Keep repeating Step 2 until you no longer have an any doubt about your answer. That is very likely your team's Core Purpose. Other ways to ask the Step 2 question are:

- Why is that relevant?
- Why does that matter?

**Step 4:** Write down what you come up with and sleep on it.

Your Core Team purpose is very likely an aha moment where you say, "Of course! That is it!" If you are not there yet, keep going. It may take some time to get it right.

## THRIVER'S WISDOM

### Safe and Heard: Linda Henry

As the first woman to lead the *Boston Globe* in its 150-year history, Linda Henry has certainly learned how to propagate and promote a healthy team environment—amid a high-pressure industry with significant responsibilities and a brand constantly in the spotlight. She's not afraid to admit she's still learning and ask for feedback, which by the way, is one of her strengths. Here, she tells you how to do it.

### Communicate Vulnerability

I'm very deliberate about saying I don't know something when I don't know something. In part I'm sure to do this because I don't want people to feel they have to be experts. There are plenty of things I know a lot about and plenty of things I don't. That doesn't mean I'm not intelligent, it just means I don't have the full picture. I'll say, "I don't understand all the rules here." For example, when can a journalist speak on a panel? I'm not the expert. I trust and empower people. I try to create an environment where it's OK to not know something. And we're all learning. I strongly believe a leader needs to set the tone and tempo of learning by saying and showing "I will learn this with you" and "help me understand this."

### Reinforce Purpose and Mission

I am so lucky to work at an organization that really, truly believes in the mission to serve our community. Our community is stronger because we have a vibrant, fully resourced newsroom. We are the largest newsroom in New England. Our newsroom is the core. We're the check on the police, the government, and city councils. This is critical for our community because more people vote and run for office when there is a strong newsroom. Local media is trusted in a way that cable television isn't. I believe so strongly in our region and there is nothing I wouldn't do to help our community to ensure we have a strong newspaper. I feel like the luckiest person in the world because I truly believe what I'm doing is the best possible thing I could be doing with my limited time on earth and the resources I have. I'm very clear to let people know we are always going to do the right thing. There is nothing more important than our credibility as an institution. I make it OK for people to do the right thing. It helps them relax. We're going to keep doing the right thing every time. There is nothing more important than honoring our mission and purpose—no amount of money, no client we need—not one thing.

## Respect Others' Time

Recently I launched an employee survey with the overarching desire to understand how best we can respect the time of each individual. In it, I made clear: "I want you to tell me what we're doing wrong and right. I want you to be part of this process because I do respect your time." I want employees to feel they have ownership, that they are very empowered and part of the decision process. I'll say, "Here is a decision we're having to make on when to reopen the office. What does it look like when we reopen? Here is what's going on with our negotiations with the union. Do you have any feedback?" My aim is for others to feel valued and respected.

## Foster Relevance and Innovation

You can't be romantic and nostalgic about what was if you are doing a real transformation. What worked before was irrelevant. It was holding us back. If you want transformation, you really have to let go of what was and look at what is. We made a lot of mistakes, but now we're running as this innovative company that takes the best ideas from everywhere. We keep shining a light on critical issues. A strong, trusted, well-resourced newspaper can have such an impact. We help change the conversation by fostering relevance and staying innovative.

## Make People Feel Safe

Leaders need to demonstrate psychological safety and make it safe for others to take risks. Celebrate. Don't emphasize, *oh, this project failed*. We've tried a lot of things that don't work. In organizations you have been with for a long time, you may have tried something 20 years ago and it didn't work, but that is completely irrelevant if everything about the current context has changed. We're going to keep trying. It's OK if it doesn't work; that to me is safety. You're safe to throw out that idea and try things, and if it doesn't work, we've learned. That is a healthy team environment.

## POWER RECAP Creating a Healthy Team Environment

### Key Points About This Practice

- Team members want you, the team leader, to make them feel part of something bigger, that you show them how what they are doing together is important and meaningful.

- Team members want you to make them feel that you can see and connect to them in their current experiences and authentic stories, care about them, and challenge them, in a way that recognizes who they are as individuals.

- Strengths-based groups communicate using a common language grounded in what's good.

- Remember that every individual retains areas where they're not strong.

- Sincerity and empathy are essential ingredients to exceptional team leadership.

- A clear direction provides team members with an anchor for their commitment to the team.

- With honest feedback, mutual respect, and personal openness encouraged, team members are more likely to report higher emotional well-being.

## Suggested Actions

- Understand and unleash team member strengths.

- Engage and clarify team purpose, vision, mission, and strategy.

- Communicate honestly and convene frequently for service excellence.

- Learn and develop together.

- Make it appreciative.

- Ensure psychological safety.

# COMMITTING TO THE WORK OF THE INCLUSIVE LEADER™

*It's my job to be an ally for all. It is critically important as a white male and a white male in power to set a model and expectations that relate to diversity and inclusion. This isn't just about being a good person. That is insufficient. Leaders make choices that drive equity, and I am learning every day how best to do this.*
—Dan Helfrich, CEO, Deloitte Consulting LLP

## DOING THE WORK OF THE INCLUSIVE LEADER

The Work of the Inclusive Leader (a framework we'll share with you later in this chapter) is imperative. Building on your best self work, understanding others and their stories is critical. While this practice focuses on setting the tone and modeling behavior for your team—whether that's several members or several thousand members—it's important to start with yourself. Doing the inner work means paying attention and being aware of your own thoughts and feelings and noticing when biases arise. It means paying attention to how others might see things and how this is likely different from how you may experience the same things. Once you really understand others, you can work together to make systemic changes and create an *inclusive culture*. This work is important for individual success, both because it's the right thing to do and because it solidifies your leadership journey. In addition, it benefits the organization because you and your colleagues are maximizing your contributions.

*Committing to the Work of the Inclusive Leader* allows you to supercharge your impact by fully engaging a diverse group of team members. Being an inclusive leader means paying attention to the individual needs of all of your stakeholders and providing them the ample tools they need to arrive and thrive. It also means being intentional about your own understanding and learning, with a focus on the biases that may be affecting your decision making, the systems you are operating in, and how you can help level the playing field. These are the skills and competencies that will be vital for arriving and thriving in the coming years.

We like this definition from inclusion scholar and author Dr. Bernardo Ferdman: "Inclusive leadership is the practice of leadership that intentionally provides ways that allow everyone across multiple types of differences, to participate, contribute, have a voice, and feel that they are connected and belong, without losing individual uniqueness or having to give up valuable identities or aspects of themselves."

In this final of our 7 Practices you will build on all of the other practices of arriving and thriving, because inclusive leadership is the knowing, the doing, and the being about who you are as a leader.

Inclusive leadership must start with the inner work on your identity, and understanding who you are as a leader, or what we call "the *knowing*." The Work of the Inclusive Leader is a lifelong, lifewide learning journey. Continual, consistent. The reason that everything starts with the knowing is that once you appreciate your own identity, you harbor a curiosity about others. Your self-assuredness allows for the murmur within that desires to know more details about another individual to become louder in tone and translate to meaningful engagement, resonance, and unity.

The *doing* is everyday leadership practices—possessing and living a strong set of values, being fair and transparent, advocacy and allyship. Consider that *every day*, we wake up and learn something different about inclusive leadership because humankind, by nature, is dynamic and evolving. Nested inside the workplace, this everyday learning and engagement inevitably leads to goals, even dreams, being fulfilled. Fulfilled dreams and goals happen because when we are consciously inclusive, we connect the unique strengths of the people we know to opportunities for them to add value. How do we facilitate inclusive conversations? How do we respect and value someone from a different background? How do we ensure people from underresourced or underrepresented backgrounds are successful? The illumination fuels the doing.

Showing up as your authentic self is the *being*. So many leaders who want to be more inclusive ask "What should I do?" And doing the right things is absolutely essential. But without showing up in an authentic way, living your values, and connecting with and caring about others, the doing is hollow and won't result in people feeling truly valued and included.

## WHY THE PRACTICE IS ESSENTIAL

Inclusive leadership results in organizational effectiveness and competitive advantage. It makes the organization, the team, and the individual better. Why? Because people are more engaged and they feel like they have a unique and important contribution to make, and that allows you to harness the power of diversity to increase creativity and innovation. Hearing from a variety of diverse voices is also the best defense against groupthink, a psychological phenomenon that occurs within a group of people in which the desire for harmony or conformity in the group results in an irrational or dysfunctional decision-making outcome. Inclusive leaders tend to make better decisions comprised of creativity, uniqueness, and independent thinking. Diverse talent and an inclusive culture led by inclusive leaders are the building blocks to truly advancing equity, which is about results: measurable and meaningful outcomes. Consider research from Deloitte underscoring that organizations with inclusive cultures perform better than organizations without inclusive cultures (Figure 7.1).

**Organizations with inclusive cultures are:**

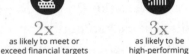

| 2x | 3x | 6x | 8x |
|---|---|---|---|
| as likely to meet or exceed financial targets | as likely to be high-performing | more likely to be innovative and agile | more likely to achieve better business outcomes |

**FIGURE 7.1** The Case for Inclusive Leadership

Source: Juliet Bourke, *Which Two Heads Are Better Than One? How Diverse Teams Create Breakthrough Ideas and Make Smarter Decisions* (Australian Institute of Company Directors, 2016).

To further encapsulate this point, we can understand why the book *INdivisible: Radically Rethinking Inclusion for Sustainable Business Results* made it as a top pick in Harvard Business School Faculty's "2021 Summer Reading List." Authors Alison Maitland and Rebekah Steele make the case that inclusive leadership matters because of performance, preparedness, and purpose. Performance is a wide range of business outcomes from those we listed previously to increased loyalty and well-being of team members. Preparedness is about helping "organizations adapt and prepare for the challenges of digital transformation," and purpose is about leveraging the "common ground between inclusion and sustainability . . . to give greater meaning and purpose to work, providing motivation for employees and building trust with stakeholders such as customers, investors, and communities."

For women leaders, there are additional benefits to leading inclusively. Sometimes women think they must go solo and that the reason that they've been successful is that they do everything themselves. Women may also suffer from the idea that it's easier to just do things themselves rather than delegating or asking for help. That is what Susan calls "over-rowing" and it's a recipe for overwhelm and burnout. She states in her book *Mastering Your Inner Critic*:

> We women need to fundamentally rethink what we are doing, how much we are doing, and ultimately how hard we are rowing at home and at work . . . not only are we exhausted, we are unintentionally alienating those around us with the waves made by our too-fast rowing, and/or we are too busy doing it all to see how much willing and eager help we could tap into to help us.

Being an inclusive leader means you don't have to be the superhero. You don't have to know everything and do everything. And actually, you can't do the work equivalent of carrying a huge boulder by yourself. Isn't that a relief? As an inclusive leader, you can focus on what you do best and partner with others who are also bringing their best to the table. Together, you will discover more creative, compelling solutions, and you'll do it from an approach that is much more sustainable. Inclusive leadership means going from the "me" to the "we" and creates a whole that is greater than the sum of its parts.

An additional aspect for women leaders is that we often face what is called the *double bind*, where society's expectations about what it means to be a woman (caring, warm, nice) conflict with society's expectation of what it means to be a leader (strong, decisive, tough). If women fail to meet either set of expectations, people of all genders will judge them more harshly than they judge men who behave in a similar fashion.

Summarized in the edifying piece "How Women Manage the Gendered Norms of Leadership" in *Harvard Business Review*, researchers have identified four common conflicts that women leaders face, all stemming from the need to be both tough and nice. They call these paradoxes:

1. Demanding yet caring
2. Authoritative yet participative
3. Advocating for themselves yet serving others
4. Maintaining distance yet being approachable

Being an inclusive leader provides you a strategy for navigating the double bind. With it, you are able to build and prioritize relationships and to care for each person according to their needs. In other words, to exhibit many of the six signature traits of the inclusive leader (see Janet's favorite tool, which follows). By increasing your competency as an inclusive leader, you can be more effective in meeting your goals and objectives in a way that minimizes the impact of the double bind.

## ACING THIS PRACTICE AND SUSTAINING YOURSELF AS A ROLE MODEL TO FOLLOW

With the help of esteemed members of its strategic advisory board, and with our insight and direction, our colleague at Simmons University Institute for Inclusive Leadership Elisa van Dam has led the development of a model that provides a road map for this practice. Called the Work of the Inclusive Leader, this model transpires at three levels: becoming aware (for yourself), becoming an ally and upstander (supporting others), and becoming a change agent (advocating for systemic change).

Within each level, there are two actions, as you can see from Figure 7.2:

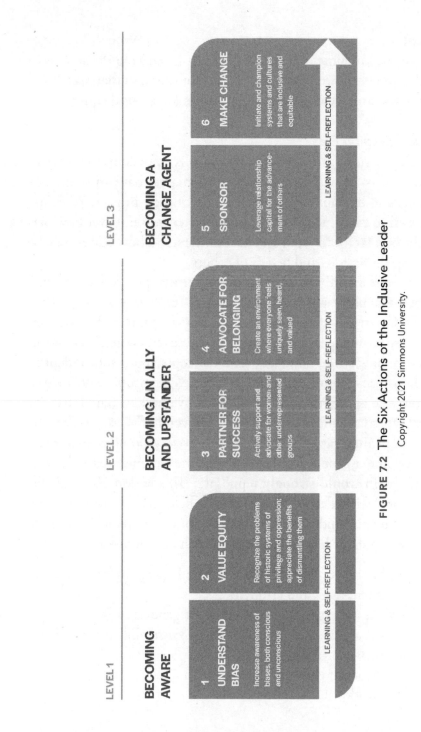

**FIGURE 7.2 The Six Actions of the Inclusive Leader**

Copyright 2021 Simmons University.

## Level 1

Part of the knowing of inclusive leadership is taking the actions in level 1 and becoming more aware, both of the ways that bias shows up for you and what your personal values are around equity.

### *Understanding Bias*

The first action under becoming aware is understanding bias in all its forms. We all have unconscious biases that can shape our actions and decisions if we aren't aware of their impact. Your first action is to examine your own belief systems to uncover how bias might be a factor for you, and also understand how biases may be shaping the actions and beliefs of others.

In corresponding leadership development programs, we often suggest that participants take one or more Implicit Association Tests (IAT). Created by Project Implicit, which was founded by three scientists specializing in social cognition, these tests were developed to measure how strongly we associate concepts about social identity (such as Black people, Asian American people, people who are gay, people who are transgender) with either evaluations (good, bad) or stereotypes (athletic, clumsy). Taking several of these tests can be an eye-opening way to start your self-discovery, pointing to implicit biases you may not be aware you have, or even ones that your conscious brain would strongly repudiate. This action also calls for intentional self-reflection. It may also be helpful to think about how to deepen your understanding of how your own identities and life experiences shape how you see others with questions like:

- What messages did I receive when I was growing up about different races and ethnicities?
- What messages did I receive about gender?
- What about sexual orientation, physical ability, and other dimensions of diversity?
- How might these messages be influencing how I see the world?

- When and how are these biases most likely to impact my decision making?

### Valuing Equity

Remember that thriving is an *advanced* state of well-being. At your vigorous level of development, the second requirement of individual understanding is comprehensive: increasing your knowledge of the history and the current context around different dimensions of diversity, including gender, race, sexual orientation, ability, and many more. (What we call "social identities.") This will deepen your understanding of how systems have historically privileged some people and oppressed others, and how those systems continue to create inequity today. Inclusive leaders must move from focusing on good intentions to focusing on good results that can be measured against a demanding standard: equity. This understanding provides a critical foundation for the other actions, helping ensure that your actions have the impact you intend and that you minimize negative unintended consequences.

There are many valuable resources, from reports like Deloitte's *The Equity Imperative* to books, podcasts, and articles that will help deepen your understanding. You can also ask trusted friends and colleagues to share their experiences with you, which is an intimate opportunity to expand your understanding of some of the common terms used by diversity, equity, inclusion, and belonging practitioners; we've provided a key terms list (see pages 175–176) to get you started. Perhaps start by reflecting on why belonging, inclusion, and equity are important to you and how they apply to your core values. You may surprise yourself!

## Level 2

In Level 2, you move from individual learning and awareness to individual action. We use the terms "ally" and "upstander" to describe this function. Technically speaking, those terms are slightly different, and understanding those differences can help point to different ways you can take action. The term upstander refers to a person who speaks or acts in support of someone else—especially if that person is being ignored or attacked. The term ally describes a person who supports the advancement of someone from a different social identity: for example, men as allies for women, or white people as allies for Black, Indigenous, Latinx, Asian American, and/or other underrepresented people. At Simmons, "allyship" is defined as using a position of power or privilege to actively support and advocate for members of underrepresented groups. In essence, as an ally, you use situations where you have unearned privilege to amplify the voices and increase the visibility of people who don't "look like" you. It can also mean educating other people who share your social identity and helping them correct biased and discriminatory behavior. Think of the impact you make in this step alone.

It's worth unpacking what we mean by "situations where you have unearned privilege." You may hear the word "privilege" and think, *that doesn't apply to me! I've often been the only woman in the room who had to fight to get my voice heard*, or maybe, *I'm a first-generation college graduate who had to work two jobs to pay my tuition. I'm not privileged!* We have certainly learned over the last sets of years that many women do have incredible privilege. However, we don't want to downplay the challenges that you have faced. They are real and important. When we talk about unearned privilege, we are referring to situations where you aren't subject to obstacles that impede people from a different underrepresented group.

For example, many of us can recall a time when we expressed an idea that was completely ignored, and then a few minutes later, a man said the same thing and was widely praised. The man didn't have any problem being heard because he was in the majority population. However, our gender created an obstacle that made our contribution invisible. Although most people in the room were likely entirely unaware of it, the man was benefiting from unearned privilege.

A fitting metaphor is that unearned privilege is like a tailwind that pushes you forward in ways you may not even recognize or notice. People who don't benefit from that unearned privilege face strong headwinds that impede their progress.

## UNDERSTANDING KEY TERMS

**Diversity** is about all the ways that human beings differ from one another. It's important to recognize that diversity includes so much more than the things we can see.

**Equity** is about systems that ensure everyone has fair access to opportunities and is treated according to their needs.

**Equality**, by comparison, is when all people are treated identically, without consideration for historical and systemic barriers and privileges.

**Inclusion** means making an effort to ensure everyone's voice is heard and leveraged so everyone feels they belong.

**Social identity** is the term we use to describe different dimensions of diversity, because they describe a person's sense of identity based on what groups they belong to.

**Micro-inequities** are the small ways that biases show up as differential treatment of people who aren't in the majority group. It might be leaving someone off of a meeting invitation or rolling your eyes when someone is talking. Each individual situation might seem inconsequential, but over time they add up—it's like drops of water wearing away a stone.

**Emotional tax** describes the consequences of being in an environment where you face the possibility of discrimination, bias, and micro-inequities. People in this situation "put their shields up" and mentally prepare themselves to deal with these issues. Of course, this preparedness is stressful and comes at a cost.

**Covering** means hiding part of who you are because that aspect of your identity tends to disadvantage you. For example, someone who is gay might not be out at work for fear of being discriminated against.

### Partner for Success

The first action in Level 2, becoming an ally and upstander, is partnering with colleagues from underrepresented groups to support their success and allow them to arrive and thrive. Using your awareness of how people and systems inadvertently (or sometimes deliberately) create obstacles for people who aren't in the majority, you can intervene in many different ways to help manage and remove those obstacles. We call this "partner for success."

Once you understand what it means to partner with someone to help them be more successful, opportunities to take action will present themselves virtually every day. Start small, experiment, and learn from your actions. Above all, make sure that you are truly partnering with the person you want to support by ensuring your actions are always grounded in an informed understanding of their ambitions and what they would find helpful.

### Advocate for Belonging

Belonging is a fundamental human need, crucial to our life satisfaction. As a result, most people need to feel like they belong at work to feel happy and be successful. A useful way to think about belonging is by considering how it interacts with another fundamental human need: to be seen as unique. As you can ascertain from Figure 7.3, you can only truly be your best self and contribute at your maximum capacity if you both are seen as unique and feel that you belong. If one of those dimensions is missing, you will feel excluded, alienated, or invisible.

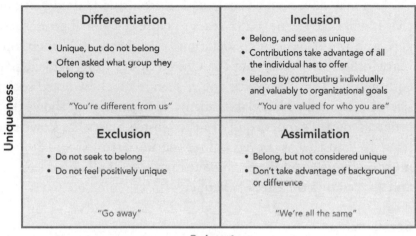

| Differentiation | Inclusion |
|---|---|
| • Unique, but do not belong<br>• Often asked what group they belong to<br><br>"You're different from us" | • Belong, and seen as unique<br>• Contributions take advantage of all the individual has to offer<br>• Belong by contributing individually and valuably to organizational goals<br>"You are valued for who you are" |
| Exclusion | Assimilation |
| • Do not seek to belong<br>• Do not feel positively unique<br><br>"Go away" | • Belong, but not considered unique<br>• Don't take advantage of background or difference<br>"We're all the same" |

Uniqueness

Belonging

**FIGURE 7.3** Uniqueness and Belonging

"Inclusion and Diversity in Work Groups," *Journal of Management*:
Shore, Randel, Chung, Dean, Ehrhart, and Singh, 2011

Being an advocate for belonging happens at the individual level. It means listening to their voice, valuing their voice, and valuing their success. Belonging encapsulates creating a community where I'm invested in you, you're invested in me, and we believe in each other's success.

The action of advocating for belonging is about creating an environment where everyone feels like they are appreciated and respected for who they are, and where they don't have to hide aspects of their identity. This practice involves creating a sense of trust and psychological safety as we discussed in Practice 6: Creating a Healthy Team Environment. It also means making sure that everyone's contributions are seen and valued.

## Level 3

*Clear vision. Patient yet persistent. Courageously asking tough questions. Knowledgeable and leads by example. Strong relationships built on trust.* Who does this sound like? A change agent.

You may have seen the calculation from the United Nations that it will take the next 257 years to close the global gender pay gap, and the American Association of University Women and many others have cited that the United States won't achieve pay equity until 2093. Or maybe you've seen research by noted social scientists from the National Academy of Sciences that shows that progress toward gender equity in the United States has slowed or stalled—and that was even before the impact of Covid-19. We must do better. And that's why our final level is all about leading and accelerating the pace of change.

### Sponsorship

The first activity of Level 3 is sponsorship, defined as "using relationship capital to support the advancement of someone else." Sponsors are generally one or more levels higher in the organizational structure than the person they are sponsoring, providing sponsors with the opportunity to be in "conversations of influence" where opportunities are discussed. As a sponsor, you put your reputation on the line to actively advocate for someone from an underrepresented group.

Writing for *Harvard Business Review*, Rosalind Chow defined sponsorship as:

> a form of intermediated impression management, where sponsors act as brand managers and publicists for their protégés. This work involves the management of others' views on the sponsored employee. Thus, the relationship at the heart of sponsorship is not between protégés and sponsors, as is often thought, but between sponsors and an audience— the people they mean to sway to the side of their protégés.

This definition then provides a useful way to identify sponsorship actions, including sharing a protégé's accomplishments, vouching for a protégé who is seeking a new opportunity, making strategic connections, and/or defending or "providing air cover" when things don't go as planned.

### Making Change

Our final action as a change agent is making organizational change, which involves initiating and driving changes in systems, policies, or procedures to level the playing field. To build an equitable future, leaders must activate the full breadth of their control and influence across all parts of their organizations and beyond: from relationships to products, services to spend, governance to external interactions—essentially three spheres: workforce, marketplace, and society (see Figure 7.4).

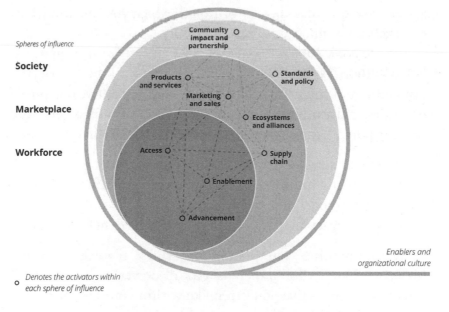

FIGURE 7.4 The Equity Activation Model

© 2021 Deloitte Development LLC

It starts by examining cultural orthodoxies and flipping those that may be getting in the way of pursuing equity. This can be at the team level, like creating norms around how meetings are run to ensure all voices are heard. This can also be at the department level or even organizationwide, like changing how performance evaluations are done to minimize the impact of unconscious biases. Although this is the highest level and most complex practice of the model, leaders at all levels (even individual contributors) can and should suggest and engage in these activities. You can lead change from any position in the organization, whether that's at the senior leadership, grassroots level, or somewhere in between.

Deloitte suggests a systems-based view for how your businesses can activate equity within and outside of their own organizations, structured around three primary spheres of influence within the reach of every organization: workforce, marketplace, and society. Each sphere, in turn, includes multiple activators—key areas of activity and everyday choices—through which your organizations can exert their influence to activate equity.

In the book *Positive Organizing in a Global Society*, Lynn and her coauthors explore how to approach this work by identifying individual and collective strengths that lead to positive outcomes, processes, and attributes of organizations and their members. As a starting point, Lynn suggests considering questions like:

- What makes employees feel like they're thriving?
- How can I bring my organization through difficult times to be stronger than before?
- What creates the positive energy a team needs to be successful?

While making change may sometimes involve organizationwide change efforts, there is a lot of power in "small wins." These are changes that you can make within your own sphere of influence that either minimize an obstacle or make it easier for everyone to have equal access. One example is changing a meeting time to make it easier for everyone to attend. Or updating a job description template to minimize the number of requirements, which has been shown to increase the number of women who apply. The great thing about small wins is that they often gain momentum and lead to larger changes across the organization.

We've addressed the significance of courageous conversations, which can arguably nestle in with all the practices described, from your leadership position. With that, doing this systems-level work—consisting of numerous principles or procedures according to your organization—means that you will need to have some courageous and fierce conversations about inclusion.

We also need mental models of change that we try, test, and learn from. Longtime educators and researchers on diversity Dr. Terrence Maltbia and Anne Power suggest that we think intelligently about systems and how systems create opportunities and barriers. This entails:

- Context and stakeholder mapping
- Conceptual clarity, having a theory of change and logic model to execute
- Informed actions through data
- Engaging continually in organizational learning

## AUTHORS' PICKS
### Our Favorite Tools and Best Advice for Committing to the Work of the Inclusive Leader™

**Janet Loves the Six Signature Traits of an Inclusive Leader**

A team at Deloitte identified the six signature traits of an inclusive leader. In doing so, we have mined our experiences with more than 1,000 global leaders, deep diving into the views of 15 leaders and subject matter experts, and surveying over 1,500 employees on their perceptions of inclusion. We have also built on existing thought leadership and applied research and drawn on work with our inclusive leadership assessment tool—on which our six-part framework is based—which has proved both reliable and valid in pilot testing. Through this extensive work, we've come to understand that inclusive leadership is about:

1. Treating people and groups fairly—that is, based on their unique characteristics, rather than on stereotypes.
2. Personalizing individuals—that is, understanding and valuing the uniqueness of diverse others while also accepting them as members of the group.
3. Leveraging the thinking of diverse groups for smarter ideation and decision making that reduces the risk of being blindsided.

To achieve these aims, highly inclusive leaders demonstrate six signature traits—in terms of what they think about and what they do—that are reinforcing and interrelated (see Figure 7.5). Collectively, these six traits represent a powerful capability highly adapted to diversity. Embodiment of these traits enables leaders to operate more effectively within diverse markets, better connect with diverse customers, access a more diverse spectrum of ideas, and enable diverse individuals in the workforce to reach their full potential.

**Trait 1:** *Commitment.* Highly inclusive leaders are committed to diversity and inclusion because these objectives align with their personal values and because they believe in the business case.

**Trait 2:** *Courage.* Highly inclusive leaders speak up and challenge the status quo, and they are humble about their strengths and weaknesses.

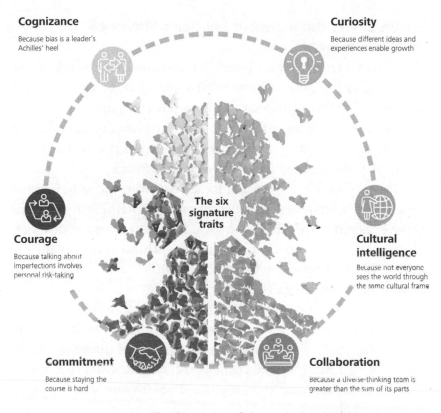

**Cognizance**
Because bias is a leader's
Achilles' heel

**Curiosity**
Because different ideas and
experiences enable growth

**Courage**
Because talking about
imperfections involves
personal risk-taking

**Cultural
intelligence**
Because not everyone
sees the world through
the same cultural frame

The six
signature
traits

**Commitment**
Because staying the
course is hard

**Collaboration**
Because a diverse-thinking team is
greater than the sum of its parts

**FIGURE 7.5** The Six Traits of the Inclusive Leader
Deloitte Insights

**Trait 3:** *Cognizance of bias.* Highly inclusive leaders are mindful of personal and organizational blind spots and self-regulate to help ensure "fair play."

**Trait 4:** *Curiosity.* Highly inclusive leaders have an open mindset, a desire to understand how others view and experience the world, and a tolerance for ambiguity.

**Trait 5:** *Culturally intelligent.* Highly inclusive leaders are confident and effective in cross-cultural interactions.

**Trait 6:** *Collaborative.* Highly inclusive leaders empower individuals, as well as create and leverage the thinking of diverse groups.

## Susan Loves the Inclusive Leader's Playbook and Assessment

One day, when Lynn and I were talking about the Work of the Inclusive Leader™, she suggested that it would make a great subject for something simple and easy for busy professionals to use. I took the idea to my colleague Elisa van Dam, the head of our Allyship and Inclusion practice. She immediately loved it, and in July of 2021, we published the *Inclusive Leader's Playbook*.

The playbook is a great tool for anyone who wants to learn to be a more inclusive leader. In addition to explaining the actions we've explored in this chapter, it includes reflection questions, suggested actions, and definitions, along with an action planning guide. The playbook is written to be a quick and fun read that demystifies what it means to lead inclusively.

In conjunction with the playbook, we have created a 360-degree leadership assessment that allows you to identify your strengths and areas of opportunity around inclusive leadership. The two together make a powerful combination that allows individual leaders and their organizations to cultivate inclusive leadership behaviors.

## Lynn Loves Capacity Building as a Learning Organization

In the book *Positive Organizing in a Global Society,* Lynn and her fellow editors offer a tool that provides leaders with a framework for five learning practices of inclusive leaders (see Figure 7.6). This tool will help you build—with intention—an inclusive learning organization. The five learning practices include:

1. **Shared vision** is the aspirational compass for directing inclusive practices. It expresses how the organization defines its current commitment to inclusion and its mantra for a better future state. Furthermore, it inspires purpose and reinforces values for inclusive leadership.

2. **System thinking** is a leader's cognitive map for understanding how stakeholders, institutions, and individuals influence inclusive actions.
3. **Mental modeling** provides conceptual clarity and logic for the inputs, transformative processes, and outputs for successful inclusive leadership.
4. **Team mastery** is the intentional collaboration of organizational members for learning inclusive practices.
5. **Personal mastery** is an individual's commitment of time and energy for learning inclusive practices.

| Shared Vision | Systems Thinking | Mental Modeling | Team Mastery | Personal Mastery |
|---|---|---|---|---|
| The organization has a shared vision for inclusion that is aligned with its current strategy and future positioning. | The organization has developed contextual awareness to understand how the macro-environment influences inclusive management practices. | The organization has conversations to identify the assumptions that influence its inclusive leadership practices and desired outcomes. | Team members invest energy In learning from each other and collective learning. | Individuals invest energy in thinking and learning about inclusion. |
| The vision outlines the purpose of why the organization manages for inclusion. | The organization has mapped its ecosystem to take into account external and internal factors for managing inclusion. | The organization is aware of its blind spots, biases, and tendencies for inclusion and exclusion of stakeholders. | Team members value differences. Teams have routines for constructively managing conflict and value dialogue. | Individuals are skilled at working with people from diverse backgrounds. |
| The vision for inclusion is consistent with the organization's values. | | The organization comprehends that individuals and groups are complex cultural beings. | Trust, mutual respect, and belonging are hallmarks of teamwork. | Individuals experiment with diverse ideas as a practice for innovating. |

**FIGURE 7.6** Capacity Building as a Learning Organization

"Diversity Management as a Generative Strategic Process: When the Business Case Meets Positive Organizational Scholarship," Positive Organizing in a Global Society: Understanding and Engaging Differences for Capacity Building and Inclusion, Wooten, L. Parson, K., Griswold, R. and Welch, S. (2016)

There are four enablers that support the creation of an inclusive learning organization:

1. **Collaborate:** invest in inclusive cultures
2. **Control:** design measurement systems for inclusive practices
3. **Create:** leverage inclusion for product and service innovation

4. **Compete:** Inclusion as a differentiator and organizational asset

| Collaborate | Control | Create | Compete |
|---|---|---|---|
| The organization's culture is inclusive of differences. Diversity management is a core aspect of the organization's human resource management practices.

To achieve its goals, the organization has a diversity of partnerships. | The organization has systems to ensure equity and equal treatment.

The culture rewards inclusive practices and there are consequences for exclusion.

There is a diversity management scorecard for goal setting and measuring performance. | The organization has a culture that recognizes and values a diversity of voices as input for innovation.

The work environment encourages entrepreneurship and experimentation.

Employees are empowered to scan the environment for opportunities. | The management of diversity is employed as an asset to broaden and build the organization's core competencies.

The management of diversity is viewed as a source of competitive advantage.

Diversity is connected to the organization's "winning proposition" for its value creating activities. |

**FIGURE 7.7** Enabling Value Creation

Wooten, L. Parson, K., Griswold, R. and Welch, S. (2016). Diversity Management as a Generative Strategic Process: When the Business Case Meets Positive Organizational Scholarship in Positive Organizing in a Global Society: Understanding and Engaging Differences for Capacity Building and Inclusion. Edited by Laura Morgan Roberts, Lynn Perry Wooten and Martin Davidson.

Since most change tools operate at the micro level (they are either very individual or interpersonal), we created this tool because we need to be thinking at the system and organization level and focus on organizational learning. This will allow us to do the work of inclusive leadership at a strategic level.

# RAISED TO BE AN INCLUSIVE LEADER: LYNN'S PERSONAL ACCOUNT

I'm so grateful that my parents inspired me to be an inclusive leader. My father was a clinical social worker and very progressive for his time. He made sure to expose me to people from different backgrounds so I could hear their stories and understand how differences add value to society. He also wanted to show me that in some ways what we perceive as differences are very much similarities. My mother taught me about the service aspect of inclusive leadership, about creating welcoming spaces so people feel like they belong. They were my first role models for inclusive leadership.

Maybe you have heard of a symbol from Ghana called "Sankofa." Sankofa is symbolized by a bird pointed forward while turning its head back. The translation of the word is "go back and get it," and the symbol is often associated with the proverb that says, "It is not wrong to go back and fetch what is at risk of being left behind." In other words, if we don't understand our history, we can't learn from it and know what we want to carry forward. I think that's what the Work of the Inclusive Leader is all about.

Professors Richard Bolden and Philip Kirk of the University of the West of England, Bristol (2009) pointed out that the relational view of leadership relates well to the collectivistic and humanist values of Ubuntu, stating that Ubuntu "bridges the 'individual' and the 'collective.'" Inclusive leadership, similar to Ubuntu, involves relational practice, collaboration, consensus building, true engagement, and creating inclusive work cultures. The major focus of both Ubuntu and inclusive leadership is on collective relational practice, the entwined nature of our relationships, and increased inclusion of interconnected systems. Ubuntu can thus be considered not only relational but also inclusive in nature and centers on the interdependence of the individual and collective.

As we said at the beginning of the chapter, this is lifelong and lifewide work. The road won't always be easy, but the rewards are immeasurable.

# LEARN, REFLECT, CONQUER CHALLENGES, AND ASCEND IN THE PRACTICE

The foundation of the Work of the Inclusive Leader is learning and self-reflection. Scholars Scott DeRue, Susan Ashford, and Christopher Myers talk about learning agility: We have to learn and then we have to quickly pivot and adapt. To do this successfully, we must have an ongoing commitment to deliberate practice and to evaluating our impact. That includes requesting, accepting and processing feedback from others on how we are doing. As we discussed in Practice 3: Cultivating Courage, having a "learning mind" and embracing a growth mindset is essential for all aspects of arriving and thriving.

As rewarding and important as the work of the inclusive leader is, we would be remiss if we didn't acknowledge that it is challenging as well. Our approach to these challenges is to look at them through the lens of positive psychology and to ask how we can build on our strengths to solve tough problems.

One aspect of this approach is Lynn's strong belief in the power of "calling in" instead of "calling out." To quote Loretta J. Ross from her piece, "Speaking Up Without Tearing Down" in *Learning for Justice*:

> Calling out happens when we point out a mistake, not to address or rectify the damage, but instead to publicly shame the offender. In calling out, a person or group uses tactics like humiliation, shunning, scapegoating or gossip to dominate others. . . . Calling in is a technique that does allow all parties to move forward. . . . Calling in is speaking up without tearing down. A call-in can happen publicly or privately, but its key feature is that it's done with love. Instead of shaming someone who's made a mistake, we can patiently ask questions to explore what was going on and why the speaker chose their harmful language. . . . Calling

in cannot minimize harm and trauma already inflicted, but it can get to the root of why the injury occurred, and it can stop it from happening again.

Ross goes on to note that calling in isn't the answer for everyone or for every circumstance. But whenever it is possible to use this technique, we believe it is far more effective and likely to result in all parties feeling better about the outcome.

On the other side of the equation, when we are the ones who have made an inadvertent misstep or been less than 100 percent successful in leading inclusively, we work hard to give ourselves grace. That means both taking responsibility for how to recover (more on that in a minute) and reminding ourselves that we are human, and we are always learning. As we stated earlier, this is a lifelong, lifewide learning process, and learning requires putting yourself in situations where you might get things wrong. (Remember our thoughts around the power of not knowing and growth mindset in Practice 3: Cultivating Courage.)

Although it's in a somewhat different context, think about Daniel Kahneman's reaction to being wrong. To reference again Adam Grant's book *Think Again: The Power of Knowing What You Don't Know*, when the Nobel Prize–winning psychologist discovers an aspect of his research or thinking that is wrong, his reaction is akin to joy: it means he's now less wrong than before.

So what do you do when you get things wrong? First, acknowledge the harm, and if you have impacted a particular person, make a sincere apology. Second, strive to learn from the experience: What happened? Why did it happen? What was the impact? What will you do differently next time? Paying attention and committing to being aware as an inclusive leader means you will need to get used to being in "learner mode" more often than not. This way of thinking (wanting to better understand from a place of assuming you don't) can and will deeply enhance your ability to manifest inclusion—and ultimately equity in leadership.

## THRIVER'S WISDOM

### *Living and Leading Diversity: Dan Helfrich*

Dan Helfrich, chairman and chief executive officer of Deloitte Consulting LLP, leads a team of more than 70,000 professionals who help clients solve their most complex problems. He is also quite the proponent of creativity, uniqueness, and independent thinking. His values and behaviors started young, which he can clearly trace, and as he clearly states in his advisory to you.

### Leverage Your Personal Story to Embrace Diversity

It comes from early in life. I came from a diverse family, including three adopted siblings, one of whom is Black. It comes from a life of being on team sports, a total melting pot of socioeconomics, class, personality, characteristics. I've been around a diverse range of people my whole life and have always seen teams that perform best when the unique aspects of all people are harnessed. As I began my professional life, I noticed professionally there were so many people mentoring and spending time with miniature versions of themselves, and I found myself seeking completely different types of people and really benefiting as mentor and mentee in those two-way relationships.

### Recognize Where Others Are and Learn Their Stories

Embrace your authentic self (Practice 2). Consider intention and ease. What I have found in my own journey and in seeing others and helping others, particularly women, is that the "ease" part is not easy. In many ways for many people, that is a practiced learned behavior versus something that is natural. The way it is revealed is in the uniqueness of each individual's—each woman's—lived experience. Does it manifest itself in people, women, carrying challenges they have from a parenting standpoint? Sure. That is a common moment when women leaders are vulnerable about the pressures they feel to "do it all." At times, the weight of that is impossible. But sometimes we equate vulnerability and authenticity with motherhood at the expense of lots of other interesting things. In fact, I've had a couple of moments stick out to me where a woman has spoken out about the decision not to have children or not to be married and articulate the pressures that creates for them. I've heard people talk about the cultural nuances, from people of Asian heritage where cultural nuances around gender and the struggles they have had to be authentic to their cultural heritage while being role models for the type of leader they want to be with our culture at Deloitte and societal culture in the United States.

## Teach Allyship

I do consider myself an ally. I don't use the word often to describe myself. I do deeply believe in the concept of allyship. The reason I don't use the word a lot myself is I believe it's my job to be an ally for all. Am I an ally for women? Absolutely. Black people? Absolutely. LGBTQ members of my team? Absolutely. Particularly as a white male, particularly as a white male in power, you are both setting a model and an expectation for the intentionality of supporting those who are different than you. If that intentionality is associated with allyship, that resonates with me. I tell our people all the time, as it relates to diversity and inclusion, it is not just OK to be a good person. Sometimes I talk to people. What are you doing to move the needle? "I have great values." "I have lots of friends who are women . . . gay . . ." "I make all my decisions in an inclusive way." My very strong statement is, that is insufficient. There has to be everyday intentionality to choices that drive equity given that many people start from positions of nonequity. It is our role to lift them up.

### Consciously Develop Your Skills as an Inclusive Leader

Without question, read, listen, and follow the most diverse set of perspectives as possible and spend time with individuals inside and outside of work that are as diverse as possible. To me, it's all about agile dynamic leadership to the situation and to the moment in society and the company. One of the best ways to make sure you don't become a leader in a castle who has lost perspective in the world or a leader in a castle surrounded by other leaders who have many of the same attributes as yourself is by choosing intentionally to spend your time with as diverse an array of people as possible.

## POWER RECAP Committing to the Work of the Inclusive Leader™

### Key Points About This Practice

- Inclusive leaders understand others and their stories.

- Being an inclusive leader means you don't have to be the superhero. You don't have to know everything and do everything.

- Hearing from a variety of diverse voices is the best defense against groupthink.

- Part of the knowing of inclusive leadership is becoming more aware, both of the ways that bias shows up for you and what your personal values are around equity.

- Becoming an ally and upstander is partnering with colleagues from underrepresented groups to support their success and allow them to arrive and thrive.

- Belonging encapsulates creating a community where I'm invested in you, you're invested in me, and we believe in each other's success.

## Suggested Actions

- Take an Implicit Association Test (IAT).

- Reflect on why belonging, inclusion, and equity are important to you, and how they apply to your core values.

- Work with the Six Signature Traits of an Inclusive Leader tool.

- Complete the *Inclusive Leader's Playbook* and Assessment.

# REFERENCES AND FURTHER READING

## FOREWORD
Emma Hinchliffe,"The female CEOs on this year's Fortune 500 just broke three all-time records" Fortune (June 2, 2021), https://fortune.com/2021/06/02/female-ceos-fortune-500-2021-women-ceo-list-roz-brewer-walgreens-karen-lynch-cvs-thasunda-brown-duckett-tiaa/.

## PRACTICE 1
Brady, S. M. (2018). *Mastering your inner critic and 7 other high hurdles to advancement: How the best women leaders practice self-awareness to change what really matters* (1st ed.). McGraw-Hill Professional.

*Business Chemistry*®. (2022). Business Chemistry | Deloitte. https://www2.deloitte.com/us/en/pages/operations/solutions/business-chemistry.html

Christifort, K. and Vickberg, S. (2018*). Business Chemistry: Practical magic for crafting powerful work relationships.* New York: Wiley.

Firestone, L. (2017, August 17). *The unselfish art of prioritizing yourself | Psychology Today.* Psychology Today. https://www.psychologytoday.com/us/blog/compassion-matters/201708/the-unselfish-art-prioritizing-yourself

Firestone, R., Firestone, L. A., & Catlett, J. (2002). *Conquer your critical inner voice: A revolutionary program to counter negative thoughts and live free from imagined limitations.* New Harbinger Publications; Distributed in the USA by Publishers Groups West.

Firestone, R. W., Firestone, L., & Catlett, J. (2012). *The self under siege.* Routledge. https://doi.org/10.4324/9780203122426

Gallup Inc. (2022a). *CliftonStrengths assessment.* Gallup.Com. https://www.gallup.com/cliftonstrengths/en/252137/home.aspx

Gallup Inc. (2022b). *What are the 34 CliftonStrengths themes?* Gallup.Com. https://www.gallup.com/cliftonstrengths/en/253715/34-cliftonstrengths-themes.aspx

*Glendon Association Staff | The Glendon Association.* (2012, May 4). The Glendon Association. https://www.glendon.org/about-glendon/glendon-staff/

Goetzel, R. Z., Roemer, E. C., Holingue, C., Fallin, M. D., McCleary, K., Eaton, W., Agnew, J., Azocar, F., Ballard, D., Bartlett, J., Braga, M., Conway, H., Crighton,

K. A., Frank, R., Jinnett, K., Keller-Greene, D., Rauch, S. M., Safeer, R., Saporito, D., . . . Mattingly, C. R. (2018). Mental health in the workplace: A call to action proceedings from the mental health in the workplace—public health summit. *Journal of Occupational & Environmental Medicine, 60*(4), 322–330. https://doi.org/10.1097/JOM.0000000000001271

Goleman, D. (2000). *Working with emotional intelligence.* Bantam Books.

Goleman, D. (2011). *The brain and emotional intelligence: New insights.* More Than Sound. http://search.ebscohost.com/login.aspx?direct=true&scope=site&db=nlebk&db=nlabk&AN=465760

Goleman, D. (2020). *Emotional intelligence: Why it can matter more than iq* (1st ed.).

Goleman, D. (2021a). *About Daniel Goleman.* https://www.danielgoleman.info/biography/

Goleman, D. (2021b). *EI assessments.* https://www.danielgoleman.info/ei-assessments/

Goleman, D., Boyatzis, R. E., & McKee, A. (2013). *Primal leadership: Unleashing the power of emotional intelligence* (Tenth anniversary edition). Harvard Business Review Press.

*How the Enneagram system works.* (2021). How The System Works. https://www.enneagraminstitute.com/how-the-enneagram-system-works

Myers, I. B. (1962). *The Myers-Briggs Type Indicator: Manual.* Consulting Psychologists Press. https://doi.org/10.1037/14404-000

*Official Myers Briggs test & personality assessment.* (2022). MBTIonline. https://www.mbtionline.com/?gclid=CjwKCAjwiY6MBhBqEiwARFSCPhmdfN1lzRhFfWvrmZJvGG--Jhi-LC-J4l-NCdfzl3OMXwx3dJHYLBoCDScQAvD_BwE

*"Positive Identities" series.* (2020).

Quinn, R. E., Dutton, J. E., Spreitzer, G. M., Roberts, L. M., Plews, E. J., & Max, J. (2010). *Reflected Best Self Exercise™.* https://reflectedbestselfexercise.com/

Quinn, R., Dutton, J., Spreitzer, G., & Roberts, L. Morgan (2011). Reflected best self exercise: Revised instructions. *Ross School of Business, Positive Organizational Scholarship Teaching Tools Series.*

Rath, T., & Conchie, B. (2008). *Strengths based leadership: Great leaders, teams, and why people follow.* Gallup Press.

Richard Safeer. (2022). *Dr. Richard Safeer.* Dr. Richard Safeer. https://richardsafeer.com/

Riso, D. R., & Hudson, R. (1996). *Personality types: Using the enneagram for self-discovery* (Rev. ed). Houghton Mifflin.

Riso, D. R., & Hudson, R. (1999). *The wisdom of the enneagram: The complete guide to psychological and spiritual growth for the nine personality types.* Bantam Books.

Riso, D. R., & Hudson, R. (2000). *Understanding the enneagram: The practical guide to personality types* (Rev. ed). Houghton Mifflin.

Roberts, L. (2020). Positive Identities: Affirm your way. Video produced by the Center for Positive Organizations, https://positiveorgs.bus.umich.edu/videos/positive-identities-affirm-your-way/.

Roberts, L. Morgan, Dutton, J.E., Spreitzer, G., Heaphy, E., & Quinn, R. (2005). Composing the reflected best self portrait: Building pathways to becoming extraordinary in work organizations. *Academy of Management Review, 30:* 712–736.

Roberts, L. Morgan, Spreitzer, G., Dutton, J., Quinn, R., Heaphy, E. & Barker, B. (2005). How to play to your strengths. *Harvard Business Review, 83(1):* 75–80.

Safeer, R., & Allen, J. (2019). Defining a culture of health in the workplace. *Journal of Occupational & Environmental Medicine, 61*(11), 863–867. https://doi.org/10.1097/JOM.0000000000001684

*Sandra L. Fenwick | Boston Children's Hospital.* (2022). Boston Children's Hospital | About Us. https://www.childrenshospital.org/about-us/our-leadership/sandra-fenwick

Simmons University. (2022). *Strategic Leadership for Women | Simmons University Institute for Inclusive Leadership.* Simmons University Institute for Inclusive Leadership. https://www.inclusiveleadership.com/courses-learning-journeys/arrive-thrive/strategic-leadership-women/

Sorenson, S. (2014, February 20). *How employees' strengths make your company stronger.* Gallup.Com. https://www.gallup.com/workplace/231605/employees-strengths-company-stronger.aspx

*The Myers & Briggs Foundation—Original Research.* (n.d.). Retrieved January 5, 2022, from https://www.myersbriggs.org/my-mbti-personality-type/mbti-basics/original-research.htm

*VIA character strengths reports | VIA Institute.* (2022). https://www.viacharacter.org/reports

## PRACTICE 2

Bell, Emma. (2016, January 20). *Why Workplace Dress Codes Have Troubled Women for Decades.* https://www.newsweek.com/high-heels-and-workplace-460312

*Brené Brown: The power of vulnerability | TED Talk.* (n.d.). Retrieved January 7, 2022, from https://www.ted.com/talks/brene_brown_the_power_of_vulnerability/transcript?language=en#t-49565

Brown, B. (2015). *Daring greatly: How the courage to be vulnerable transforms the way we live, love, parent, and lead* (First trade paperback printing). Avery.

George, B., McClean, A. and Craig, N. (2008*). Finding Your True North: A Personal Guide.* Jossey Bass.

George, B., & Sims, P. (2007). *True north: Discover your authentic leadership* (1st. ed.). Jossey-Bass.

Gillard, J. (2019). *Julia Gillard: My story.* Penguin Books Australia.

Harris, Carla (2020). Differentiate Yourself. YouTube, https://www.google.com/search?q=carla++harris+differentiate+yourself&source=lnms&tbm=vid&sa=X&ved=2ahUKEwiWyu_P88_1AhUdkYkEHQoYCDsQ_AUoA3oECAEQBQ&biw=3840&bih=1432&dpr=1.

Harris, C, (2017). Being Smart Isn't Enough. YouTube, https://www.youtube.com/watch?v=j-5hR9YeSyo.

Harris, C. A. (2010). *Expect to win: 10 proven strategies for thriving in the workplace.* Plume.

Harris, C. A. (2014). *Strategize to win: The new way to start out, step up, or start over in your career.* Hudson Street Press.

Hewlett, Sylvia Ann, Leader-Chivée, Lauren, Sherbin, Laura, Gordon, Joanne, & Dieudonné, Fabiola. (2013). *Executive Presence.* Coqual.

Ibarra, H. (2015a). *Act like a leader, think like a leader.* Harvard Business Review Press.

Ibarra, H. (2015b, January 1). The Authenticity Paradox. *Harvard Business Review.* https://hbr.org/2015/01/the-authenticity-paradox.

Simmons University Institute for Inclusive Leadership (2021). 2021 Leadership Development Survey, https://www.inclusiveleadership.com/app/uploads/2021/07/The-Importance-of-Authenticity-in-the-Workplace.pdf

Smith, C., & Yoshino, K. (2019). *Uncovering talent: A new model of inclusion* (p. 20). Deloitte. https://www2.deloitte.com/content/dam/Deloitte/us/Documents/about-deloitte/us-about-deloitte-uncovering-talent-a-new-model-of-inclusion.pdf

## PRACTICE 3

Ashford, S. J., & Detert, J. R. (2015, January 1). Get the boss to buy in. *Harvard Business Review*. https://hbr.org/2015/01/get-the-boss-to-buy-in

Bloom, L., & Bloom, C. (2018, July 9). *Beware of the perils of confirmation bias*. Psychology Today. https://www.psychologytoday.com/us/blog/stronger-the-broken-places/201807/beware-the-perils-confirmation-bias

Bourke, J. (2016, April 14). *The six signature traits of inclusive leadership*. Deloitte Insights. https://www2.deloitte.com/us/en/insights/topics/talent/six-signature-traits-of-inclusive-leadership.html

Brady, S. M. (2018). *Mastering your inner critic and 7 other high hurdles to advancement: How the best women leaders practice self-awareness to change what really matters* (1st ed.). McGraw Hill Professional.

Brown, B. (2012). *Daring Greatly: How The Courage To Be Vulnerable Transforms The Way We Live, Love, Parent, and Lead*. Penguin/Gotham.

Brown, B. (2010, June). *The power of vulnerability*. TedX. https://www.ted.com/talks/brene_brown_the_power_of_vulnerability

Byrnes, J. P. & Miller, D. C. & Schafer, W. D. (1999). Gender Differences in Risk Taking: A Meta-Analysis. *Psychological Bulletin*, Vol 125(3). https://psycnet.apa.org/buy/1999-13573-004?mod=article_inline

Charness, G., & Gneezy, U. (2012). Strong evidence for gender differences in risk taking. *Journal of Economic Behavior & Organization*, 83(1), 50–58. https://doi.org/10.1016/j.jebo.2011.06.007

Covin, R. (2011). *The need to be liked*. Amazon.

Dai, J. (2021, April 1). *AT&T business CEO Anne Chow reflects on leadership, discrimination as an Asian-American woman*. The Cornell Daily Sun. https://cornellsun.com/2021/04/01/att-business-ceo-anne-chow-reflects-on-leadership-discrimination-as-an-asian-american-woman/

Deloitte Insights. Human Inside: How capabilities can unleash business performance, https://www2.deloitte.com/content/dam/insights/us/articles/6799_cultivating-and-nurturing-human-capabilities/DI_Cultivating-and-nurturing-human-capabilities.pdf.

Detert, J. R. (2021). *Choosing courage: The everyday guide to being brave at work*. Harvard Business Review Press.

Dorsey, C., Kim, P., Daniels, C., Sakaue, L., & Savage, B. (2020). Overcoming the racial bias in philanthropic funding. *Stanford Social Innovation Review*. https://doi.org/10.48558/7WB9-K440

Dweck, C. S. (2006). *Mindset: The new psychology of success* (1st ed). Random House.

Gulamhussena, M. and Santa, S. (2015). Female directors in bank boardrooms and their influence on performance and risk-taking. *Global Finance Journal*, 28: 10-23

Grant, A. M. (2021). *Think again: The power of knowing what you don't know*. Penguin Random House.

Grant, H. (2018). *Reinforcements: How to get people to help you.* Harvard Business Review Press.

Hagel, III, J., Wooll, M., & Brown, J. S. (2020, June 26). *Human inside: How capabilities can unleash business performance.* Deloitte Insights. https://www2.deloitte.com /us/en/insights/focus/technology-and-the-future-of-work/building-capability -unleash-business-performance.html

Harris, C. R., Jenkins, M., & Glaser, D. (2006). Gender differences in risk assessment: Why do women take fewer risks than men? *Judgment and Decision Making, 1*(1), 16.

Keizer, G. (2009) *Help: The original human dilemma.* Harper One.

Klaver, M. N. (2007). *Mayday! Asking for help in times of need* (1st ed). Berrett-Koehler Publishers.

Lieder, R. (2018, May 11). Leading a purposeful team. *Richard Lieder Blog.* https:// richardleider.com/leading-a-purposeful-team/

Liu, E. M., & Zuo, S. X. (2019). Measuring the impact of interaction between children of a matrilineal and a patriarchal culture on gender differences in risk aversion. *Proceedings of the National Academy of Sciences, 116*(14), 6713–6719. https://doi.org/10.1073/pnas.1808336116

McCarthy, K. (2019, September 5). *AT&T Business names Anne Chow 1st female CEO.* ABC News. https://abcnews.go.com/Business/att-business-names-anne-chow-1st -female-ceo/story?id=65408600

Miao, C. (2019). Peer Effect and Risk Aversion. Econ 196 Honors Thesis, University of California—Santa Barbara. https://escholarship.org/content/qt9ts40903 /qt9ts40903.pdf

Natalie Martinez. (n.d.). *Strong Women Strong Girls.* Retrieved January 6, 2022, from https://swsg.org/about/team/natalie-martinez/

Roosevelt, E. (1960). *You learn by living: Eleven keys for a more fulfilling life* (1st ed.). Harper.

Roosevelt, T. (1910). *The Man in the Arena,* https://www.theodorerooseveltcenter.org /Learn-About-TR/TR-Encyclopedia/Culture-and-Society/Man-in-the-Arena.aspx.

*Strong Women Strong Girls: Our story.* (2022). https://swsg.org/about/our-story/

Warrell, M. (2015). Asking for Help is a Sign of Strength Not Weakness, https:// margiewarrell.com/asking-for-help-is-a-sign-of-strength-not-weakness/.

Wilson, L. (2018, September 13). *Asking for help may be a privilege.* CivicScience. https://civicscience.com/asking-for-help-may-be-a-privilege/

## PRACTICE 4

Cross, R., Dillon, K., & Greenberg, D. (2021, January 29). The Secret to Building Resilience. *Harvard Business Review.* https://hbr.org/2021/01/the-secret-to -building-resilience

Ellin, A., & Young, A. (2020, December 17). Special report: Why developing resilience may be the most important thing you can do for your well-being right now. *Everyday Health.* https://www.everydayhealth.com/wellness/state-of-resilience/

Fisher, J., & Phillips, A. N. (2021). *Work better together: How to cultivate strong relationships to maximize well-being and boost bottom lines.* McGraw Hill.

Human Capital. (2021, August 19). *Whitney Johnson On S-Curve Theory.* https://www .youtube.com/watch?v=NS7aB5q4IQs

James, E. H., & Wooten, L. P. (n.d.). *Promoting Resilience*. James+Wooten. Retrieved January 7, 2022, from https://jamesandwooten.com/promoting-resilience/.

James, E & Wooten, L. (2010). *Leading Under Pressure: From Surviving to Thriving Before, During, and After a Crisis*. New York: Routledge Academic Press.

Johnson, W. (2012). *Dare, dream, do: Remarkable things happen when you dare to dream*. Bibliomotion.

Johnson, W. (2018). *Build an A-team: Play to their strengths and lead them up the learning curve*. Harvard Business Review Press.

Johnson, W. (2019). *Disrupt yourself: Master relentless change and speed up your learning curve*. Harvard Business Review Press.

Johnson, W. (2022). *Smart growth: How to grow your people to grow your company*.

Luders, E., Cherbuin, N., & Gaser, C. (2016). Estimating brain age using high-resolution pattern recognition: Younger brains in long-term meditation practitioners. *NeuroImage, 134*, 508–513. https://doi.org/10.1016/j.neuroimage.2016.04.007.

Ngô, T.-L. (2014). Revue des effets de la méditation de pleine conscience sur la santé mentale et physique et sur ses mécanismes d'action. *Santé Mentale Au Québec, 38*(2), 19–34. https://doi.org/10.7202/1023988ar

Pascale, R. T., Sternin, J., & Sternin, M. (2010). *The power of positive deviance: How unlikely innovators solve the world's toughest problems*. Harvard Business Press.

Pradhan, B., & Gogineni, R. (2018). Mind, Mindfulness, and the Social Brain: Psychobiological Understandings and Implications. *Indian Journal of Social Psychiatry, 34*, 313–322.

Rogers, E. M. (1962). *Diffusion of Innovations*. Free Press of Glencoe.

Safeer, R., & Allen, J. (2019). Defining a culture of health in the workplace. *Journal of Occupational & Environmental Medicine, 61*(11), 863–867. https://doi.org/10.1097/JOM.0000000000001684.

Safeer, R., & Allen, J. (2019). Defining a culture of health in the workplace. *Journal of Occupational & Environmental Medicine, 61*(11), 863–867. https://doi.org/10.1097/JOM.0000000000001684

Sood, A. (2020, December 14). 20 tips for building and cultivating your resilience. *Everyday Health*. https://www.everydayhealth.com/wellness/resilience/top-tips-help-build-cultivate-resilience/

Sutton, J. (2021, December 12). Positive Deviance: 5 Examples Of The Power of Non-Conformity. *PositivePsychology.Com*. https://positivepsychology.com/positive-deviance/

Veenstra, J., & Chisesi, K. (n.d.). Building resilience: How C-suite executives can not only bounce back, but bounce up from adversity. *Deloitte Perspectives*. Retrieved January 7, 2022, from https://www2.deloitte.com/us/en/pages/about-deloitte/articles/building-resilience-roadmap-for-the-modern-csuite.html.

Wooten, L. & James, E. (2008). Linking Crisis Management and Leadership Competencies: The role of Human Resource Development. *Advances in Human Resource Management Development*, 10(3): 352–379.

Wooten, L. & Johnson, W. (2021). Fireside Chat on Resilience and Disrupting Yourself: Simmons University Institute for Inclusive Leadership. Conference Report: Inspiring Resiliency and Authenticity. Simmons Institute for Inclusive Leadership, https://www.inclusiveleadership.com/app/uploads/2021/06/2021_ConferenceInsights_FNL.pdf.

**PRACTICE 5**

*2021 Global marketing trends.* (2021). 80.

Brady, S. M. (2018). *Mastering your inner critic and 7 other high hurdles to advancement: How the best women leaders practice self-awareness to change what really matters* (1st ed.). McGraw-Hill Professional.

Cohn, A. (2018, April 4). *Premier women's leadership expert Sally Helgesen teaches women how to rise.* Forbes. https://www.forbes.com/sites/alisacohn/2018/04/04/premier-womens-leadership-expert-sally-helgesen-teaches-women-how-to-rise/

Deloitte. (2021). *Global 2021 millennial and gen z survey.* 39.

Deloitte (S. Kounkel, A. Silverstein, K. Peeters) (2021). Global Marketing Trends: Find Your Focus. https://www2.deloitte.com/content/dam/insights/us/articles/6963_global-marketing-trends/DI_2021-Global-Marketing-Trends_US.pdf (Pages 6–13)

*Deloitte Digital.* (2021). https://www.deloittedigital.com/

*Discover The Five Practices of Exemplary Leadership*®. (2022). https://www.leadershipchallenge.com/research/five-practices.aspx

Dufu, T. (2017). *Drop the ball: Achieving more by doing less* (First edition). Flatiron Books.

Friedman, S. D. (2008, April 1). Be a better leader, have a richer life. *Harvard Business Review.* https://hbr.org/2008/04/be-a-better-leader-have-a-rich-life

Ibarra, H., & Obodaru, O. (2009, January 1). Women and the vision thing. *Harvard Business Review.* https://hbr.org/2009/01/women-and-the-vision-thing

Kouzes, J. M., & Posner, B. Z. (2017). *The Leadership Challenge: How to make extraordinary things happen in organizations* (Sixth edition). John Wiley & Sons, Inc.

Kouzes, J. M., & Posner, B. Z. (2022). *Leadership Practices Inventory | Leadership Challenge.* https://www.leadershipchallenge.com/lpileadershippracticesinventory

Sinek, S. (2009a). *Start with why: How great leaders inspire everyone to take action.* Portfolio.

Sinek, S. (2009b, September). *Transcript of "How great leaders inspire action."* TEDxPuget Sound. https://www.ted.com/talks/simon_sinek_how_great_leaders_inspire_action/transcript

Sinek, S. (2019). *The infinite game* (1st Edition). Portfolio.

*The Leadership Challenge*®: *Leadership Development Solutions.* (2022). https://www.leadershipchallenge.com/home.aspx

**PRACTICE 6**

Atlassian.com. (2022.) Special Report: Openness Predicts a Team's Strength. https://www.atlassian.com/practices/open/research

Clifton, J., & Harter, J. K. (2021). *Wellbeing at work: How to build resilient and thriving teams.* Gallup Press.

*DNA of engagement: How organizations can foster employee ownership of engagement.* (2017). The Engagement Institute. https://www.conference-board.org/topics/dna-of-engagement

Dvorak, N., Deweese, C., & Ott, B. (2018, November 30). Why CliftonStrengths® Helps Managers Lead Winning Teams. *Gallup.* https://www.gallup.com/workplace/245093/why-cliftonstrengths-helps-managers-lead-winning-teams.aspx

Edmondson, A. (1999). Psychological Safety and Learning Behavior in Work Teams. *Administrative Science Quarterly, 44*(2), 350–383. https://doi.org/10.2307/2666999

Edmondson, A. C., & Mortensen, M. (2021, April 19). What Psychological Safety Looks Like in a Hybrid Workplace. *Harvard Business Review.* https://hbr.org/2021/04/what-psychological-safety-looks-like-in-a-hybrid-workplace.

Flynn, B. (2020). *Further, faster: The vital steps that take the guesswork out of growth.* Lioncrest.

*Guide: Identify what makes a great manager.* (n.d.). Google re:Work. Retrieved January 7, 2022, from https://rework.withgoogle.com/guides/managers-identify-what-makes-a-great-manager/steps/introduction/

*Guide: Understand team effectiveness.* (n.d.). Google re:Work. Retrieved January 7, 2022, from https://rework.withgoogle.com/guides/understanding-team-effectiveness/steps/introduction/

Harter, J., & Mann, A. (2017, April 12). The Right Culture: Not Just About Employee Satisfaction. *Gallup.* https://www.gallup.com/workplace/236366/right-culture-not-employee-satisfaction.aspx

Lencioni, P. (2002). *The five dysfunctions of a team: A leadership fable* (1st ed.). Jossey-Bass.

*New research: Openness predicts a team's strength.* (n.d.). Atlassian. Retrieved January 7, 2022, from https://www.atlassian.com/practices/open/research

Rath, T. (2007). *StrengthsFinder® 2.0.* Gallup Press.

*Simon Sinek: How great leaders inspire action | TED Talk.* (n.d.). Retrieved January 7, 2022, from https://www.ted.com/talks/simon_sinek_how_great_leaders_inspire_action/transcript?language=en

Sinek, S. (2011). *Start with why: How great leaders inspire everyone to take action.* Portfolio Penguin.

Sinek, S. (2017a). *Find your why: A practical guide to discovering purpose for you or your team.* Portfolio/Penguin, an imprint of Penguin Random House, LLC.

Sinek, S. (2017b). *Leaders eat last: Why some teams pull together and others don't* (Paperback edition). Portfolio/Penguin.

Sinek, S. (2019). *The infinite game* (1st Edition). Portfolio/Penguin.

Stratton-Berkessel, R. (2010). *Appreciative inquiry for collaborative solutions: 21 strength-based workshops.* Jossey-Bass.

*The Practical Magic of "Thank You."* (n.d.). Deloitte. Retrieved January 7, 2022, from https://www2.deloitte.com/us/en/pages/about-deloitte/articles/time-to-rethink-employee-recognition-strategy.html

Volini, E., Schwartz, J., Denny, B., Mallon, D., Van Durme, Y., Hauptmann, M., Yan, R., & Poynton, S. (n.d.). *2020 Global Human Capital Trends Report.* Deloitte. Retrieved January 7, 2022, from https://www2.deloitte.com/cn/en/pages/human-capital/articles/global-human-capital-trends-2020.html

## PRACTICE 7

Bolden, R., & Kirk, P. (2009). African leadership: Surfacing new understandings through leadership development. *International Journal of Cross-Cultural Management, 9*(1), 69–86.

Booysen, L. (2013). Societal power shifts and changing social identities in South Africa: Workplace implications. *South African Journal of Economic and Management Sciences, 10*(1), 1–20. https://doi.org/10.4102/sajems.v10i1.533

Bourke, J. (2016, April 15). Six signature traits of inclusive leadership | Deloitte Insights. *Deloitte Insights.* https://www2.deloitte.com/us/en/insights/topics/talent/six-signature-traits-of-inclusive-leadership.html

Chow, R. (2021, June 30). Don't Just Mentor Women and People of Color. Sponsor Them. *Harvard Business Review.* https://hbr.org/2021/06/dont-just-mentor-women -and-people-of-color-sponsor-them.

Deloitte, (2016) Six Signature Traits of an Inclusive Leader. https://www2.deloitte .com/us/en/insights/topics/talent/six-signature-traits-of-inclusive-leadership.html

Deloitte. (2022). *The equity imperative.* Deloitte United States. https://www2.deloitte .com/us/en/pages/about-deloitte/articles/the-equity-imperative.html

DeRue, D. S., Ashford, S. J., & Myers, C. G. (2012). Learning Agility: In Search of Conceptual Clarity and Theoretical Grounding. *Industrial and Organizational Psychology, 5*(3), 258–279. https://doi.org/10.1111/j.1754-9434.2012.01444.x

England, P., Levine, A., & Mishel, E. (2020). Progress toward gender equality in the United States has slowed or stalled. *Proceedings of the National Academy of Sciences, 117*(13), 6990–6997. https://doi.org/10.1073/pnas.1918891117

Explainer: Everything you need to know about pushing for equal pay. (2020, September 14). *UN Women.* https://www.unwomen.org/en/news/stories/2020 /9/explainer-everything-you-need-to-know-about-equal-pay

Ferdman, B. M., Prime, J., & Riggio, R. E. (Eds.). (2020). *Inclusive leadership: Transforming diverse lives, workplaces, and societies.* Routledge/Taylor & Francis Group.

Grant, A. M. (2021). *Think again: The power of knowing what you don't know.* Viking.

MacKenty Brady, S., & van Dam, E. (n.d.). *The inclusive leader's playbook: The work of the inclusive leader.*

Maitland, A., & Steele, R. (2020). *INdivisible: Radically rethinking inclusion for sustainable business results.* Young & Joseph Press.

Maltbia, T. E., & Power, A. T. (2009). *A leader's guide to leveraging diversity: Strategic learning capabilities for breakthrough performance* (1. ed). Butterworth-Heinemann.

*Project Implicit.* (2011). https://implicit.harvard.edu/implicit/user/pih/pih/index.jsp

Roberts, L. M., Wooten, L. P., & Davidson, M. N. (Eds.). (2016). *Positive organizing in a global society: Understanding and engaging differences for capacity building and inclusion* (First Edition). Routledge, Taylor & Francis Group.

Ross, L. J. (2019, Spring). Speaking Up Without Tearing Down. *Learning for Justice, 61.* https://www.learningforjustice.org/magazine/spring-2019/speaking-up -without-tearing-down

Schwab, K., Crotti, R., Geiger, T., Ratcheva, V., & World Economic Forum. (2019). *Global gender gap report 2020 insight report.* World Economic Forum.

Shore, L. M., Randel, A. E., Chung, B. G., Dean, M. A., Holcombe Ehrhart, K., & Singh, G. (2011). Inclusion and diversity in work groups: A review and model for future research. *Journal of Management, 37*(4), 1262–1289. https://doi.org/10.1177 /0149206310385943

*The Gender Pay Gap.* (n.d.). American Association of Unviersity Women. Retrieved January 10, 2022, from https://www.aauw.org/issues/equity/pay-gap/

*The Work of the Inclusive Leader.* (2022). Institute for Inclusive Leadership. https:// www.inclusiveleadership.com/courses-learning-journeys/allies-inclusive-leaders /work-inclusive-leader/

Zheng, W., Kark, R., & Meister, A. (2018, November 28). How women manage the gendered norms of leadership. *Harvard Business Review.* https://hbr.org/2018/11 /how-women-manage-the-gendered-norms-of-leadership

# INDEX

## SUSAN MacKENTY BRADY
Deloitte Ellen Gabriel Chair for Women and
Leadership; CEO, Simmons University Institute
for Inclusive Leadership

As CEO, Susan MacKenty Brady has implemented a vision for making practical and clear what it means to lead inclusively and to collaborate with and convene the most innovative thinkers, inspiring voices, and forward-thinking organizations to manifest gender parity and equity in organizational leadership—and in our lifetime. As an expert in working with technical-focused leaders and the advancement of inclusive leadership, Susan advises executives on how to create equity in leadership and works with highly accomplished leaders in ways that help them lead from their best self in the top job.

Featured on ABC's *Good Morning America*, Susan is the author of *Mastering Your Inner Critic and 7 Other High Hurdles to Advancement: How the Best Women Leaders Practice Self-Awareness to Change What Really Matters* (McGraw Hill, November 2018) and *The 30-Second Guide to Coaching Your Inner Critic* (Linkage, 2014). She is also a coauthor of the *Inclusive Leader's Playbook*. A celebrated speaker and executive coach, Susan educates and ignites leaders globally on fostering a mindset of inclusion and self-awareness.

Prior to joining Simmons University, Susan founded the Women in Leadership Institute™ and launched a global consulting practice for Linkage, Inc., on Advancing Women Leaders where she led the field research behind the 7 Leadership Hurdles Women Leaders Face in the Workforce™. Dedicated to inclusively and collaboratively inspiring every girl to realize her full potential, Susan serves as an emeritus board member of the nonprofit Strong Women, Strong Girls.

## JANET FOUTTY
### Executive Chair of the Board, Deloitte US

Janet Foutty is executive chair of the board for Deloitte US, the largest professional services organization in the United States. Janet has held this role since 2019 after serving as chair and CEO of Deloitte Consulting LLP. Janet is also a member of Deloitte's Global Board of Directors and chair of the Deloitte Foundation.

While CEO of Deloitte Consulting, she led the digital transformation and growth of the $10 billion business through significant investments in digital, artificial intelligence, and cloud. Janet previously led Deloitte's Federal and Technology businesses, which achieved exponential growth through organic growth, acquisitions, and the launch of numerous businesses, including Deloitte Digital.

Janet is a frequent author and public speaker. She regularly communicates with executive-level audiences about the changing business landscape, leadership, corporate governance, crisis resiliency, equity, and technology disruption. Janet is a passionate advocate for equity and inclusion (DEI) in the workplace; women in technology; and the need for science, technology, engineering, and mathematics (STEM) education. She has founded Women in Technology groups in India and the United States, which have seen continual growth and commitment for over a decade. Janet has steered Deloitte's DEI efforts and is committed to purposeful leadership and recognizes that business can and should make a broader societal impact that matters.

Throughout her career, Janet has served on a number of not-for-profit boards. She currently serves as chair of Bright Pink, a nonprofit dedicated to young women's health; and Business Vice-chair of the Council on Competitiveness, a nonpartisan group focused on the competitiveness agenda for the United States to attract investment, develop talent, and spur the commercialization of new ideas. Janet also serves as a board member of Catalyst, the advisory board of Columbia Law School's Millstein Center for Global Markets and Corporate Ownership, and the NYU Stern Tech Advisory board.

Janet holds a Bachelor of Science from Indiana University, and a Master of Business Administration in finance from the Kelley School of Business at Indiana University. She is an inductee of the Kelley School of Business Academy of Alumni Fellows and a member of the Kelley School of Business Dean's Council.

## LYNN PERRY WOOTEN
### President, Simmons University

A seasoned academic and an expert on organizational development and transformation, Dr. Lynn Perry Wooten became the ninth president and first African American to lead Simmons University on July 1, 2020. Specializing in crisis leadership, diversity and inclusion, and positive leadership—organizational behavior that reveals and nurtures the highest level of human potential—Lynn is an innovative leader whose research has informed her work in the classroom and as an administrator.

She first joined a university faculty in 1994 and has served in administrative roles since 2008. Lynn came to Simmons from Cornell University, where she was the David J. Nolan Dean and

Professor of Management and Organizations at the Dyson School of Applied Economics and Management. She also has had a robust clinical practice, providing leadership development, education, and training for a wide variety of institutions.

Lynn is the co-author of *Leading Under Pressure: From Surviving to Thriving Before, During, and After a Crisis* (2010) and co-editor of *Positive Organizing in a Global Society: Understanding and Engaging Differences for Capacity Building and Inclusion* (2016). Also, she has authored nearly 30 journal articles and more than 15 book chapters.

A graduate of North Carolina Agricultural and Technical State University, where she earned a Bachelor of Science in Accounting, Lynn also holds a Master in Business Administration (MBA) from the Duke University Fuqua School of Business, a doctorate in business administration from the University of Michigan Ross School of Business, and a certificate in advanced educational leadership from the Harvard University Graduate School of Education.

Lynn began her career as an assistant professor at the University of Florida Warrington College of Business. In 1998, she returned to the University of Michigan, where she was on the faculty of the Ross School of Business for nearly 20 years and served as co-faculty director of the Center for Positive Organizations, co-faculty director of the Executive Leadership Institute, and senior associate dean for Student and Academic Excellence. She departed from the University of Michigan in 2017 for the deanship at Cornell. Lynn is also a member of several national volunteer leadership organizations and is actively involved in the Boston philanthropic and civic community.